Kinship and the Drum Dance
in a Northern Dene Community

the circumpolar research series

Kinship
and the Drum Dance
in a Northern Dene
Community

Michael Asch

Published by:
The Boreal Institute for Northern Studies
Academic Printing & Publishing

The Boreal Institute for Northern Studies
ISBN 0-919058-73-6 (cloth)
ISBN 0-919058-74-4 (paper)

ISSN 0838-133X - The Circumpolar Research Series

Academic Printing & Publishing
ISBN 0-920980-38-4 (cloth)
ISBN 0-920980-39-2 (paper)

©1988 The Boreal Institute for Northern Studies

Design by O. Sanderson
Photographs by Michael Asch
Cover photo of Jessie Hardisty

Table of Contents

A Dene Account of
How the World Was Created — 1

Chapter One
A Geographic and Historical Description
of the Pe Tsʼéh Kį́ Region — 5

Chapter Two
Economic Life — 15

Chapter Three
Social Structure and Organization — 35

Chapter Four
Kinds of Music and
Instruments in Pe Tsʼéh Kį́ — 59

Chapter Five
The Social Organization
of the Drum Dance — 63

Chapter Six
The Music of the Dene Drum Dance — 73

Chapter Seven
On the Meaning of the Drum Dance — 89

Postscript
A Perspective from 1988 — 95

Appendix A
Transcription of a Song — 99

Appendix B
    Melodic Sketches   *101*
Appendix C
    Implications of Dene Kinship   *105*
    for the Structuralist Paradigm
Appendix D
    Some Conclusions on Music Analysis   *107*

References Cited   *109*

Preface

This book is based on fieldwork undertaken between August 1969 and July 1970 in the community of Pe Tsʼéh Kį́ (Wrigley),[1] Northwest Territories and first reported in my doctoral dissertation (Asch 1972). Because of the long delay between the initial research and this monograph, I have published on a number of related topics. Of this material the most comprehensively discussed aspects relate to the economic and the historical (Asch 1976, 1977, 1981, 1982). Still, much of the data contained here has not been reported in published form. Due to circumstances pertaining most directly to priorities for research during and after the Mackenzie Valley pipeline hearings (or Berger Commission), aside from a brief note on each subject (Asch 1975a, 1980), I have not written anything on the social organization of the community nor its Drum Dance music. Consequently, the material in this book, while providing an account of information collected in the late 1960s, is nonetheless "new."

When re-examining materials with the benefit of fifteen years of hindsight, it is difficult to avoid revisions and I did succumb somewhat to this temptation. Although I have not added to the database from more recent experiences of fieldwork, I have undertaken some revision to my discussion of the data. Also included here is a revision of a paper, based on my 1969-70 fieldwork, which was presented at the 1975 annual meeting of the American Folklore Society (Asch 1975b). This paper, incorporated as Chapter 7, discusses the question of what a successful Drum Dance signifies to the community of Pe Tsʼéh Kį́: a subject not covered in the dissertation. The incorporation of this paper as a chapter in this book has enabled me to re-orient the focus of the text from a treatise on ethnomusicological methodology to one which highlights the internal dynamics of economic and social stress and its resolution (particularly via the Drum Dance) at a time prior to the development of a sophisticated political response.

The primary objective of the dissertation, however, was to examine an approach to the analysis of music sound using the Slavey Drum Dance as the data base. In brief the argument developed there (but omitted from this text) was that one crucial problematic of ethnomusicology is the analysis of the sound of music appropriate to the particular culture from which it is derived; that is, an understanding of the elements of sound significant to a culture. A central purpose of my fieldwork was to examine one approach to this question. My orientation arose out of Merriam's ideas as presented in his seminal book *The Anthropology of Music* (1964) and his other work (1963, 1967) as well as from the work of McAllester (1954) and Blacking (1967). It followed an approach that I would label "Anthropological Musicology" in that, in contrast to the "Comparative Musicology" approach developed by Kolinski (1957, 1965, 1967), it firmly takes into account the cultural basis for what is considered to be music. As Merriam stated (1967:27): "...music [sound] depends upon pitch and rhythm, but only as these are agreed upon by members of the particular society."

The difficulty with any approach that tries to develop a culturally appropriate framework is that, while music sound depends upon agreement among members of a culture, most frequently the members of the culture will not discuss music in those terms and, indeed, it is often impossible to elicit any such information from them.[2] Therefore, one must try an indirect approach to attain this objective. The anthropological musicology orientation at the time of my fieldwork, especially as it had been developed by Merriam, relied exclusively on the use of the verbal accounts of community members. These accounts typically discussed what Merriam called the "use" of the music (such as "Owl Dance Song," i.e. a song used for Owl Dancing). Thus, the analyst was suggesting that all of the songs referred to as "Owl Dance Songs" by a member of the community have certain music properties in common.

The results of this analysis (and in particular its development in Merriam 1967) were not promising. That is, there seemed little correspondence between the categories (such as "Owl Dances") as developed by the community members and the music sound associated with them. In 1972, I suggested that the problem lay not in the approach itself (that is, the attempt to find culturally relevant cues) but in the way in which these cues had been derived.

> As linguists have discovered, merely because an informant can be assumed to "understand" and use his language, it does not follow that he must be consciously aware of his knowledge or capable of discussing it. In fact, informant statements most frequently describe linguistic and other phenomena in terms which are irrelevant to or even incompatible with the goals of the investigation and, in some instances, may be faulty or in error. In consequence any referent framework derived exclusively from informant statements cannot be relied upon to be relevant to the analysis. (Asch 1972:9)

For this reason I decided to rely on the extent to which the kind of social activities that took place during a Drum Dance song (rather than the verbal statements) were related to its music sound and, in particular, its tonal range, melodic structure, and/or rhythmic structure. The frame of reference was derived from my interpretation of the late 1960s anthropological linguistic model for the analysis of the structure of a language (Lyons 1969).

Looking at it in hindsight this approach, as it was applied to the Slavey Drum Dance, did not resolve the issue. On the one hand, there was some correspondence between particular aspects of music sound and social behaviours associated with particular types of dances. These findings are contained in the body of the text. They represent a re-analysis of my published results (Asch 1975a). Furthermore, the linguistic analogy itself seemed productive with respect to thinking about music and some of my thoughts on this matter (which formed the Conclusion of the dissertation) are included as Appendix D. On the other hand, the analogy in general and the approach developed in the dissertation in particular seems very weak and tenuous when compared to an anthropological linguist's analysis of language. In other words, the results seemed to indicate that using behavioural elements was more appropriate than relying on informant verbalizations alone. However, this indirect element did not in itself provide a secure purchase from which a culturally sensitive analysis of music sound could develop.[3]

The chapter on social organization, which has undergone a major revision, generally recapitulates the data presented in the dissertation.[4] The revision pertains to the model by which the kinship terminology and band organization of Pe Tséh Kį is discussed. The analysis here relies particularly on the use of a principle of binary opposition, based on the presumption that the social reality of Pe Tséh Kį is better described by Dumont's (1953) idea of "Dravidian-type" kinship than the ideas of Spier (1925) and Helm ([MacNeish] 1960, 1961). This has led me to consider certain implications for the typology of social systems as developed in Lévi-Strauss's (1969) *The Elementary Structures of Kinship* and elsewhere. In particular, I see the possibility that the social system found in Pe Tséh Kį (which I would describe as "Bilateral-Dravidianate") can be added as a fourth distinct type to the "elementary," "Crow-Omaha," and "complex" structures already described by Lévi-Strauss. A discussion of this possibility appears in Appendix C. Aside from incorporating information from fieldnotes and observations not included in the dissertation, the remaining change is the abbreviated conclusion on music analysis.

Acknowledgements

The successful completion of this research required the help and cooperation of a network of individuals and institutions so large that it would be impossible to thank them all by name here, but a few must be singled out for special mention. Without the financial support of the National Institute of Mental Health of the Department of Health, Education and Welfare of the United States of America (grant number 1-T01-MH-12060-01 CUAN) this project could not have been realized. Thanks must also be extended to Father Posset of the Roman Catholic Hostel in Fort Simpson; the Government of the Northwest Territories, which provided much logistical and practical support; and the Folklore Division of the Museum of Man, National Museums of Canada in Ottawa for a grant-in-kind of recording tapes. I would also like to thank David Lubell for providing the map of the Pe Tsʼéh Kį́ region, Henry Klumpenhower for the rendering of my musical transcriptions, Regula Qureshi for her original renderings of the transcripts and reading of this manuscript, Judith Abbott for her patience and expertise in typing the manuscript into the computer at The University of Alberta, Phil Howard and Sarah Cleary for their assistance in presenting the Slavey text in an appropriate orthography, to Nick Crangle for the trapping statistics contained in Table 2.3, the Dene Mapping Project for the land use trails, Ottilie Sanderson for her design, and to Betsy Warland, Nancy Gibson, and Laura Hargrave for their judicious and sensitive editing of the manuscript. Finally, to the people of Pe Tsʼéh Kį́ as a whole; to Wilson Pellissey, Andrew Root and the other drummers; to Edward Hardisty, Chief in 1969; to Julian Yendo, Ted Trindell, Philip and Cecilia Tale, Philip Moses, Jean Boots, Adele Hardisty, Caroline Pellissey, Marie Hansetti, and especially Jessie Hardisty go my deepest and warmest thanks for their kindness and patience with my wife, Margaret, and myself.

Footnotes

1. The Dene have asserted that the communities (and other place names) within their homeland (which they call Denendeh) should be named in the Dene languages. Using a recently developed orthography, the term the Wrigley people use to name the town of Wrigley is "Pe Tsʼéh Kį́" or, in transliteration "house (or trading post) by the big rock." In this book, I will refer to the community by its Slavey name.

2. In this sense, in music *emic* analysis (or analysis that relies on the perceptions of the members of the cultural community rather than *etic* analysis that relies on the framework of the analyst's community [see Harris 1964:8-18]) differs from much other emic analysis for in most other cases one can always rely on the verbal cues as a significant element in the analysis.

3. Others, including Blacking (1971), Feld (1974), Herndon (1971), McLeod and Herndon (1980), Nattiez (1975), have all worked in one way or another with the linguistic analogy with similar results. That is, none has found the approach which, of itself, yields the crucial indirect element. Nonetheless, these results seem to indicate the possibility that the linguistic approach may be appropriate. Qureshi's (1981) analysis of Qawwali music in India has gone a bit further, for her analysis is truly an appropriate "grammar" of music. She was, however, working in a context in which people do discuss music sound directly and in a highly sophisticated manner. In this situation she was able to utilize behaviour as a means to enrich as well as validate important components of the analysis.

4. These data have been published only as a summary piece (Asch 1980) in which some of the implications for modeling Dene social organization are discussed briefly.

A Dene Account of
How the World Was Created

recorded August 1969
(translated by E.H., August 1969)

There was a world too before. But people then were just like ministers or something like the people out in Jerusalem. But something happened and the world changed over.

Something happened and what little bit that was living was left they all gathered. But they were stuck right there, they didn't know what to do. Those few human beings and other living things gathered around and asked themselves what they could do. What could be done. But in the end they said to one another "let's find that lost world."

They were picking someone who was able and they were trying to find that lost world. That's what they were working on. Animals, one or two of each, were living. But they were left out with no land, just like on top of water.

They wanted to get somebody to find land again. They all tried, but they didn't ask the little muskrat yet. So they finally asked the rat. And you know the muskrat has got very small hands. He went down and brought up a little handful of clay. After this he continued working on it and it started getting bigger and getting bigger. Everything started to multiply and the earth started getting bigger. As it was getting bigger and bigger, well the distance got too big.

You know he's got small hands. Well as soon as he brought up this little bit of earth, well they start working on it, you know. So it got bigger and bigger and bigger, bigger and bigger. Well sometime they thought it was big enough. But to get from one end to the other the distance was too big, too great to travel. So that's where the wolf comes in.

They sent the wolf out to see how quick he can go around the world they were working on. It took one day for the wolf to get from the starting point to get back. The second time the wolf went around. Well, this time, he didn't get back until late evening.

So they gathered all around again and they talked it over. So they sent the wolf to go around again. The wolf left early in the morning. In the evening he didn't get back. During the night he never got back, but he got back the next day. When the wolf made the third trip they were glad because the earth was getting bigger. They sent him out a fourth time. This time it took the wolf two days and two nights. The fifth time the wolf went out, he didn't get back until the evening of the tenth day. They were still talking about it and they figured that the world was big enough.

In the olden days, the animals that live around here used to live like people. The best uniform that one person had was that of the old crow. When the world was finishing, they gathered all around again. They were going to make colours for things. Like the birds and waterfowl, even ducks, what colour they have, well it was the old crow who did the painting or decorating of them.

In them days, the crow was the smartest person. You can ask him to do anything and he'll do it. It doesn't matter if it's hard or easy. He just goes ahead and does it. This old crow wanted a woman. This woman was really white. He couldn't do nothing about it because the old crow he was black. This woman that the old crow wanted, she didn't want a black man to be her husband. But the old crow didn't like that. They had a curtain inside the tent so this woman wouldn't be seen by anyone until she gets married.

After they finish developing the world, well it's just like nowadays, people visiting one another in home made boats and that. But this woman there, the one who the old crow wanted to marry, she wouldn't have anything to do with anyone. The old crow, if he wanted to do anything, well it wasn't anything for him to do it, he's always got something coming up anyway. He's got a lot of boys (I mean his people). People respect him because he's like that (capable of doing anything). He got them all together for them to decorate him all in white.

After they got him all decorated up with nice groomed hair and everything. Got him all fixed up. Now he's ready to take the boat and see this woman. The other tribe that the old crow was going to see was a big tribe. Kids were playing outside. They seen a boat coming down the river and this crow he has an old tanned hide really white. He's got it spread out in the boat. He's got his feet up and he's taking it easy.

That woman's brother, as soon as they stopped down there, the boy ran down to the boat and as soon as he seen this boat all in white he didn't say nothing. He told his mom before he went "boat coming in." So he ran down to check the strangers. But as soon as he seen this guy there all in white, he didn't say nothing but he beat it back to his house. This boy came running in and told his mother "Segheh, Segheh (my cross-cousin or my brother-in-law) is coming." The bride-to-be, this old lady there, had some tanned hide all white. No dirt on it, just like a carpet. They rolled it down to the boat and up to the house. He walked up and right into the woman's house.

He's married and the old lady's happy and the brother-in-law is happy. When night came everybody went to bed. This young woman who got married with the old crow there who was decorated. They went to bed. This old crow he was reckless. He just got up.

This young lady she was all white. This old crow, he was black but he was decorated. When they went to bed he started rubbing against the woman. She got all black. Later, the old lady went behind the curtain to check on her daughter because she never sleeps that long. This old crow went "caw caw" and took off.

When this old lady found her daughter was all black she was mad. She tried to wipe off the black but she was already painted and you can't change it.

Like now we Indians are all of different colour. The black people outside, they're darker than us. Maybe the same thing happened there. This old crow in them days, he was the smartest fellow. He could make anything. Everything that was supposed to be changes or decorated he did the thinking. So that's where the world started all over again and the crow did everything. They used to talk about it not just down here but up there too - like heaven.

Chapter One

A Geographic and Historical Description of the Pe Tséh Kĺ Region

Physical Description of the Region

The town of Pe Tséh Kĺ is located in the upper basin of the Mackenzie River Valley on the east bank of the Mackenzie River at a point about 241 kilometers north of Fort Simpson and the same distance south of Fort Norman. The Dene call this community "Pe Tséh Kĺ" or, in transliteration from Slavey, "house (or trading post) by the big rock." The big rock refers to a hill located on the east bank of the Mackenzie River some 10 kilometers north of the present community. It may well have been the same hill on which Mackenzie found the remains of a Dene encampment during his voyage (Lamb 1970:179, 181).

The main topographical feature of the river valley between Fort Simpson and Fort Norman is Camsell Bend, a point about 121 kilometers north of Fort Simpson where the river makes a sharp turn and shifts from a westerly to a northerly flow. South of this point the land adjacent to the river is extremely flat and low. The land bordering both banks becomes increasingly rugged and steep to the north of this spot, until about 16 kilometers north of Pe Tséh Kĺ where the mountains approach the river from both sides. Beyond this point the mountains on the east side gradually recede from the river and the river bank becomes more level. The mountains to the west close in on the river and the bank remains rugged and steep at least as far north as Fort Norman.

At Pe Tséh Kĺ both river banks are quite a bit higher and steeper than at Fort Simpson. Looking beyond the west bank one can find the foothills of the Mackenzie Range, which ultimately extend west and north into the Yukon. To the east is the McConnell Range of the Franklin Mountains, beyond which is a region of flat and low bush land with many lakes. The town of Pe Tsɛ́h Kı̨́ itself is located behind the rather steep east bank of the river on a level and sandy plateau about sixty meters above.

The climate of the Mackenzie basin is continental (Dawson 1947:43). Winters are long and cold, lasting about five months. Summers are about three months long and are surprisingly mild. Spring and fall are periods of rapid transition which last about two months each (Kendrew and Currie 1955:77).

Map 1.1   Pe Tsɛ́h Kı̨́ and Environs

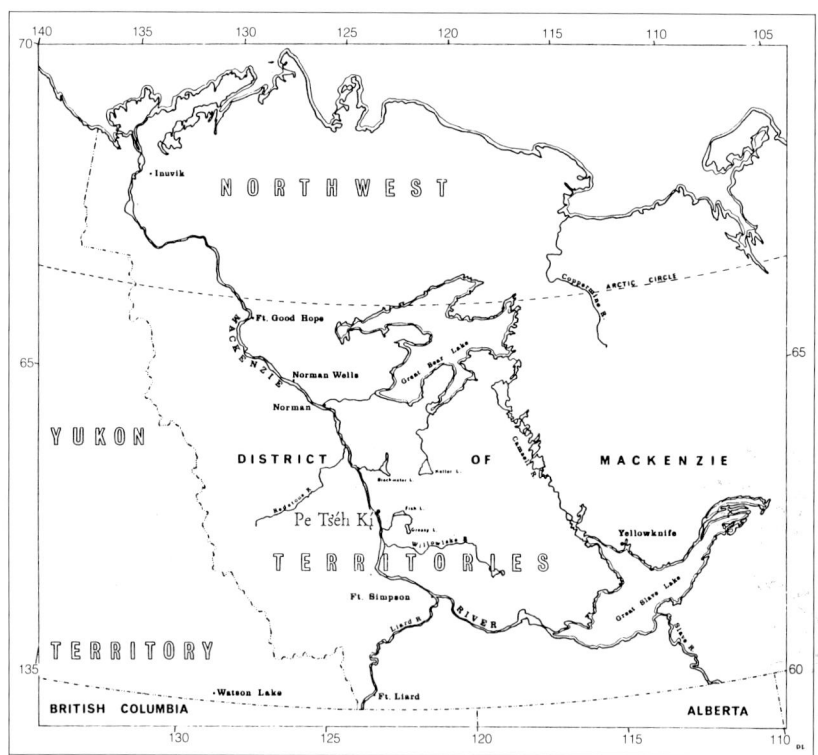

At Fort Simpson (Lat. 61° 52'N, Long. 121° 15'W, Alt. above M SL415 ft.), the nearest town to Pe Tsɛ́h Kı̨́ (Lat. 63° 14'N, Long.

123° 27'W, Alt. above M SL347 ft.) with published climatological records, the Mackenzie River freezes up at the beginning of November and remains solid until late March. During this period the mean daily temperature remains near or below -17°C and the sun shines for only a few hours a day. Snowfall averages between 1.16 and 1.27 meters annually, with most occurring during the early part of the winter. There are few blizzards and winds tend to stay below 20 k.p.h.

Pe Tséh Kį́ in winter

As the daylight hours increase between late March and early May, the river ice begins to melt and the temperature rises rapidly (at Fort Simpson the mean daily temperature rises from -17°C in March to -4°C in April to +7°C in May). Breakup occurs in early May and the river remains open until late September. During this period the mean daily temperature remains above 4°C, with daily highs going into the low 20s in June, July, and August, but dropping to 4-5°C after dark. Days are long and there are few storms. In October the temperature takes a rapid downward plunge (+8°C in September to -2°C in October to -15°C in November), sunshine decreases and the river starts to freeze up (Kendrew and Currie 1955:71, 74, 87, 94).

Pe Tsʼéh Kį́ lies in the Mackenzie lowlands section of the boreal forest region as defined by W.E.D. Halliday (1937:13). Here,

> The prevailing forest cover appears to be coniferous with white spruce the major dominant, forming pure associations. Extensive fires have, however, favoured the Alaska white birch with the species, and the appearance of jack pine associations on the lighter soil. On the better-drained alluvial soil such as old river banks, well developed stands of balsam and poplar are very characteristic, and the poorer-drained sites support numerous shallow black spruce and tamarack swamps, and large variants of wild hay meadows and willow scrub.

Summer provides a short but intense growing season for a wide variety of plant life, including such berries as saskatoons, rosehips, strawberries, raspberries, and cranberries as well as such flowers as wild rose, orchid, and bluebell. During winter, most plant life remains dormant although, on occasion, especially if the snowfall has been light, cranberries can be found as late as December.

The region is inhabited by many varieties of animal life. These include mammals such as bear, beaver, caribou, fox, lynx, marten, mink, moose, muskrat, otter, porcupine, rabbit, squirrel, wolf, wolverine; fish including, among others, trout, jackfish, loche, whitefish, and "conni" (inconnu); and such birds as ptarmigan (especially in winter) and wild chickens. In the spring migrating ducks and geese pass through the district on their way to summer nesting sites. May, June, and especially July are the months of greatest insect activity, the most noticeable varieties being the mosquito and the black fly.

Historical Note [1]

People speaking various Athapaskan languages have been in continual occupation of the upper basin of the Mackenzie River Valley for at least 3000 years (Willey 1966:411f). According to Osgood (1936:4, 15, 17), in late precontact times, people speaking both Slavey and Mountain varieties of Athapaskan inhabited the region of the Mackenzie River Valley between Fort Simpson and Fort Norman. Today, due to the movement of Mountain Indians westward across the continental divide and the expansion of Slavey speakers north and west along the river valley in the past 200 years (Osgood 1936:15, 17), the Dene in this region, including those at Pe Tsʼéh Kį́, all speak the Slavey language.

Little is known about the pattern of Athapaskan life during aboriginal times. However, even without direct archaeological evidence, it can be reasonably assumed that the people lived a nomadic hunting and gathering existence. Most scholars have agreed that their social organization consisted of small units, called "bands" (MacNeish 1956:5). Membership within a band was apparently determined through bilateral descent and bilocal residence (MacNeish 1960:287f).

In 1789, Sir Alexander Mackenzie made the first confirmed European contact with the Dene, near what is now Fort Norman, when he encountered a party of five families of Slavey and Dogrib Dene (McDonald 1966:50). Soon after his journey, fur traders established trading posts along the river including one at Fort Simpson in 1804 and one at Fort Norman in 1810 (Dawson 1947:170). They were followed in the mid-nineteenth century by missionaries from both the Anglican and Roman Catholic Churches. In 1877 the Hudson's Bay Company trading post and Anglican Mission station (Bompas 1888:37) were established along the river between Fort Simpson and Fort Norman. Known first as "Little Rapid," this point was renamed "Wrigley" after the visit of Commissioner Joseph Wrigley to the Mackenzie River District in 1878 (Hudson's Bay Company, n.d.). In 1921, the Government of Canada made treaty with the Dene of the Mackenzie River Valley, gradually assuming political and juridical control over the territory.

During the Second World War, the United States and Canadian military authorities established airfields along the Mackenzie River Valley. In 1967, legal jurisdiction over the region was transferred from the federal government in Ottawa to a territorial government headquartered in Yellowknife. By 1969, a winter road and a telecommunication line (including telephone) had been constructed along the east bank of the Mackenzie.

Since the discovery of oil north of Fort Norman in 1920 there has been extensive exploration for natural resources throughout the region. This led to the discovery of uranium in Great Bear Lake in 1930, gold near Great Slave Lake in 1934, and oil in the Fort Simpson area after the war.

Since the establishment of the settlement on the east bank of the river near the confluence of the River-Between-Two-Mountains, Pe Tséh Kí has been moved twice. In 1904, an island sandbar blocked the approach to the town; the combination of inaccessibility and disease (Hudson's Bay Company, n.d.) resulted in the first move. The trading post was now located approximately forty kilometers downstream and on the west bank of the river, where it remained until 1967 (Dawson 1947:170). In 1944, the settlement was described by Taylor (1947:65f) as follows:

> There is only one imposing building in Wrigley, the post office and radio station, a two-and-a-half-storey frame house painted white. It is supplied with a prominent wind-motor propeller used to charge batteries for transmitting radio messages. Some distance along the cutbank to the north is a pretty little Catholic Church, built of sawn planks with a shingle roof. It has a belfry and a porch at the south end, but is only occasionally opened for service. Somewhat isolated at the north end are four log cabins, with a few elevated 'caches' and some tents. Here many of the Indians of the post spend the summer, and there are about seventy-seven Indians in the immediate district. There is a similar cluster of Indian shacks at the south end of the settlement. The jungle of grass, raspberry, canes, willow, and poplar, pressed close on the settlement in midsummer, and almost impedes the path at the north end of the post.

During the Second World War an airstrip was built along the east bank of the Mackenzie River sixteen kilometers south of Pe Tséh Kį́. After the war, with the establishment of regular air service and the contemplated construction of a winter road and telecommunication line along the east bank, the Canadian government decided that the settlement should be moved to the east bank where these facilities would be more accessible. The Dene of Pe Tséh Kį́ agreed and a new town was built along the winter road and telecommunication line, about five kilometers north of the airstrip, in the summer of 1966.

Population Statistics

Statistics for the Pe Tséh Kį́ area in 1890 show a population of 164 individuals, of which, it can be estimated, at least 150 were Dene (Russell 1898:160). Following the smallpox and influenza epidemics of the early twentieth century (cf. Waldo 1923) the number of Dene declined sharply to 91 persons in 1931 (Bethune 1937:48) and to only 77 by 1941 (Dawson 1947:230). In the period since the war, due to compulsory inoculation programs for young people against European illness, the Dene population has risen dramatically. The population of Pe Tséh Kį́ during the period 1969-70 was approximately 150 persons; of these about 120 were Dene and about 30 were Euro-Canadian.[2]

The Euro-Canadian community consisted of five families and one single adult male who lived alone. The reason for their presence in the settlement was to fill certain positions requiring specific technical skills for which local people had not been trained. These positions included: power plant operator (and part-time government administrator), lower grade school teacher (1-3), upper grade teacher (4-6), airport manager, air radio operator, airport mechanic, and Hudson's Bay company post manager.[3]

The Dene community was made up of sixteen household units. Fourteen of these consisted of a couple and their unmarried children. The remaining two each consisted of a widow living with one grandchild.

The Dene population of Pe Tsʼéh Kį́ conformed to the following age-sex pyramid pattern.

Table 1.2 Age-Sex Pattern of Pe Tsʼéh Kį́ in 1970

	Male	Female
10 and under	7	15
11-20	14	20
21-30	14	5
31-40	5	5
41-50	7	8
51-60	6	2
61-70	3	3
71 and over	3	3
Totals	59	61

The Euro-Canadians lived as a separate entity, geographically isolated from the Indian population. Social contact between the groups was limited and usually restricted to job-oriented duties.

The plan of the town in 1969-70 is given in Map 1.2, page twelve.

12 • Chapter One

Map 1.2   Pe Tséh Kį́ Town Plan

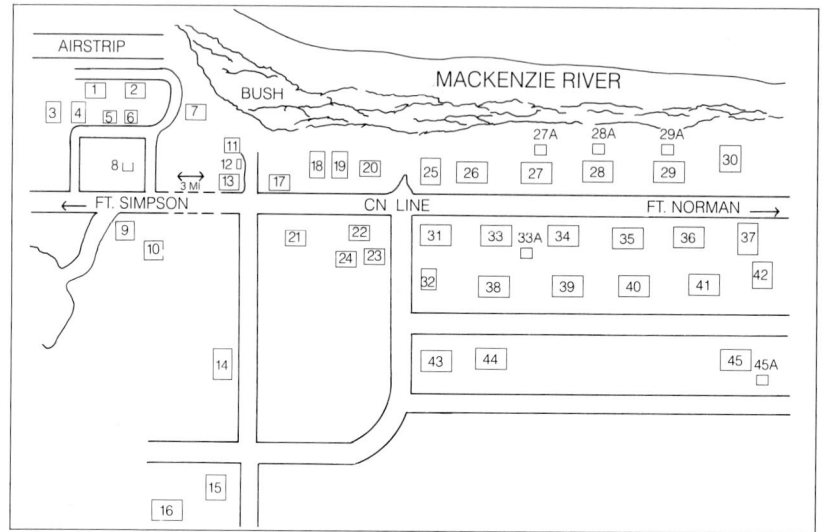

Legend

1. Department of Transport (DOT) house: occupied by Dene family.
2. DOT house: occupied by Euro-Canadian family.
3. DOT house: occupied by Euro-Canadian family.
4. DOT house: occupied by Euro-Canadian family.
5. DOT radio shack.
6. DOT storehouse.
7. DOT garage and warehouse.
8. DOT radio beacon.
9. Canadian National - Canadian Pacific (CN-CP) telecommunications repeater shack.
10. DOT shack.
11. Forestry house: unoccupied.
12. Community freezer.
13. Government (NWT) house: occupied by Indian family.
14. Forestry warehouse.
15. Government power plant and garage.
16. Government warehouse.
17. RCMP trailer: unoccupied.
18. Hudson's Bay Company (HBC).
19. HBC store.
20. HBC house: unoccupied.
21. Community hall.
22. Department of Education: lower grade school.
23. Department of Education: upper grade school.
24. Department of Education: ice skating rink.
25. Government house: occupied by Euro-Canadian family.
26. Government house: occupied by Euro-Canadian family.
27. Dene house: occupied by Dene family.
27a. Living shack belonging to family in 27.
28. Dene house: occupied by Dene family.
28a. Living shack belonging to family in 28.

29. Dene house: occupied by Dene family.
29a. Living shack belonging to family in 29.
30. Mission house belonging to Evangelical Church: unoccupied.
31. Government house: occupied by Euro-Canadian family.
32. Government house: occupied by Euro-Canadian male.
33. Dene house: occupied by Dene family.
33a. Living shack belonging to family in 33.
34. Dene house: occupied by Dene family.
35. Dene house: occupied by Dene family.
36. Dene house: occupied by Dene family.
37. House: unoccupied (but owned by a Dene family).
38. Dene house: occupied by Dene family.
39. Dene house: occupied by Dene family.
40. Dene house: occupied by Dene family.
41. Dene house: occupied by Dene family.
42. Dene house: occupied by Dene family.
43. Roman Catholic Church and Mission: unoccupied.
44. Dene house: occupied by Dene family.
45. Dene house: occupied by Dene family.
45a. Living shack belonging to family in 45.

Footnotes

1. Although more historical information is now available, the focus of the book is on the ethnographic, not historical, situation, and has therefore not been incorporated in this chapter. For recent information on Slavey Dene history as well as an up-to-date discussion of the literature, see Asch (1981), Janes (1983), Krech (1984) or the bibliographies by Helm (1973) and Helm and Kurtz (1984). For the Dene as a whole, see the volume on the subarctic in the recent Handbook of North American Indians (Helm 1981), Watkins' (1977) edited volume on Dene life in the colonial period, and Fumoleau's two recent contributions (1977, 1984).

2. The wife of one Euro-Canadian was Cree and Chipewyan. However, as she was raised in a convent, married a Euro-Canadian, and raises her children in a Euro-Canadian environment, she and her children were included within the Euro-Canadian community.

3. The position of school superintendent and airport worker were filled by Pe Tsʼéh Kį́ Indians.

Chapter Two

Economic Life

The household, of which there are fourteen in Pe Tsʼéh Kį́, is the primary economic unit. Although there are variations, which will be discussed below, a typical household is composed of a senior married couple, their unmarried children and, on occasion, their daughters' children. The economy of each household is based primarily on hunting, fishing, trapping, and cash income from wage labour and transfer payments. The household in Pe Tsʼéh Kį́ is like a subsistence family farm in that economic security depends on an adequate supply of resources from the non-cash sector and minimal demands for resources from the cash sector. This chapter outlines how the members of the community obtain their resources, the cycle of daily life, and the ways in which the subsistence needs are fulfilled, beginning with a discussion of the actual material requirement.

Housing

Each Dene household has a permanent town dwelling.[1] Fifteen of these sixteen houses were built by the government according to the same specifications.[2] They are constructed of wood, with logs for the exterior walls and side board for the interior. Each house contains a living room with kitchen area, three bedrooms and a storage closet, laid out as the illustration on the following page indicates. In the kitchen area, the government has provided permanent cabinets, a counter and a sink, and shelves for the storage area. There is no running water, but each house is wired for electricity. The house size is approximately 26' x 42'. Thirteen of the fourteen households occupy their town dwellings; one lives at the airport, leaving one town house unoccupied.

With some minor variations, all houses are similarly furnished. Immediately obvious is a ninety-gallon water barrel by the front door. The living room contains a table, chairs, and a wood stove. In the kitchen is a cookstove and, by the rear door, a wood box. The largest of the three bedrooms contains a double bed, a chest of drawers, and a stool or chair. If there is a baby, a crib or hammock also may be in this room. In the other two bedrooms are one or two cots, single beds, or wooden bed platforms as well as a chest of drawers and chair.

The house also contains cutlery, dishes, cooking utensils, meat drying equipment, bedding, and other goods related to the maintenance of the household; all of these belong to the Dene.

Figure 2.1 House Plan

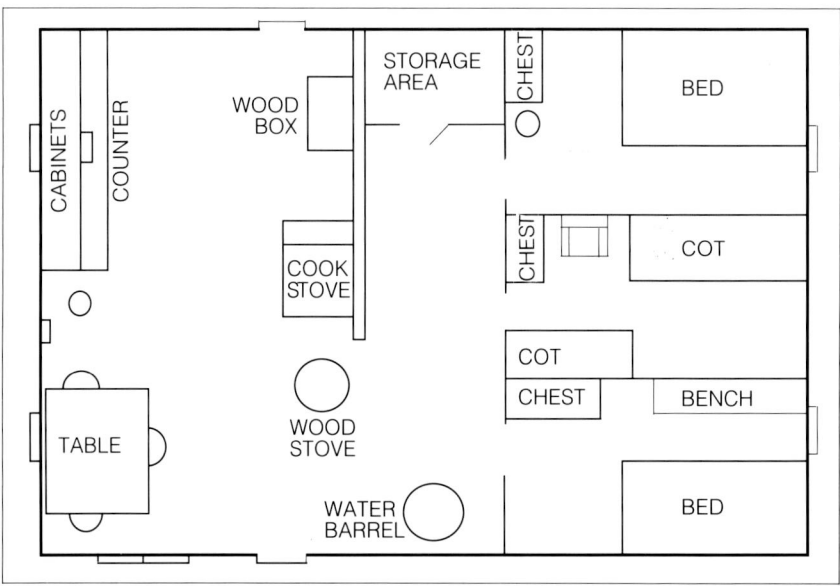

Each house is set on a lot approximately 101' x 200'. In addition these grounds contain an outhouse, a woodpile area, and a dog area. Most households also have a meat-smoking area, a storage shed or shack in which unmarried adult males live. These shacks are constructed of sideboard and usually consist of a single room with one or two beds or sleeping platforms, a heating stove and/or a cookstove, and perhaps a small closet area. The size and shape of these shacks vary greatly, depending upon the number of persons to be housed and individual taste. The lot plan varies somewhat with each household although most follow the same general arrangement.

Tanning a hide beside a shack

In addition to the town dwelling, many of the adult males have a bush shack for use during the trapping season. These shacks, constructed of logs or sideboards, greatly resemble the shacks on the house lots in town.

Clothing

Typically, clothing is bought ready-made or home-made from purchased materials. The exceptions are moccasins and some men's gloves, which are made from moosehide, and snowshoes, which are made of wood and moose sinew.

Men's clothing generally consists of a flannel shirt, a pair of work pants, a jacket or a parka, depending on the season, and a cap. Women's clothing consists of a skirt, a blouse, a sweater or shawl, a headscarf and a jacket or parka. Both men and women wear long undergarments the year round.

Children's attire, with some exceptions, follows the pattern of the adults. The boys, for example, do not usually wear caps, while the girls will often wear pants instead of a dress or skirt. Neither will wear long undergarments in the summer. Infants wear cotton diapers and baby clothes. Often they will be bare chested, something which never occurs in the case of adults or older children.

Food

The main meat staples of the Pe Tsʼéh Kį́ Slavey diet are rabbit and fish, supplemented by wild chicken. These staples account for perhaps half of the total protein intake. Other foods, such as moose and caribou, especially in the spring and fall; birds, such as ptarmigan in the winter and duck and goose in the spring; and bacon, weiners, and tinned meat, purchased from the store, provide occasional variety to the diet.

The basic starch staple is bannock, a baked mixture of flour, lard, and baking powder, which appears at most meals and is a major snack food for children. Other sources of starch are bread, oatmeal (especially for breakfast), and occasionally potatoes. These are all purchased from the Bay store.

Lard, the primary source of fat, is either purchased or obtained by rendering animal fat, and is used as a spread on bread and bannock or in cooking. Additional nutrients are wild berries in the summer, and tinned fruits in the winter, eaten either with a meal or as a snack. Tea, water, and tinned milk mixed with water for babies, are the only major beverages. Sugar is used as a sweetener in tea and occasionally with certain foods. Dogs are fed a gruel made from food scraps, dog food obtained from the Bay store, or fish.

All foods except tinned meat, tinned fruit, berries, bread, tinned milk, sugar, and lard are prepared by cooking. The basic cooking techniques are boiling, frying, roasting, drying, smoking, and baking. *Boiling* is used to prepare moose, caribou, fish, rabbit (occasionally, weiners, muskrat, beaver, potatoes, tea, oatmeal, and tinned milk for babies).

Frying is used for moose (cut into thin strips), caribou (cut into thin strips), rabbit, fish, bacon, and wild chicken. *Roasting* is used to cook chicken, duck, goose, and ptarmigan. *Drying*, an indoor technique using heat derived from the stove, is used to prepare moose, caribou, and fish. *Smoking*, a technique using heat derived from a spruce log fire, is used to prepare moose, caribou, and fish. *Baking* is used for bannock and cake.

Transportation

The mode of transportation depends upon the season, although short trips, such as to rabbit snares, are usually made on foot.

Fixing a scow and 'kicker'

In the summer (mid-May to October 1) the only form of transportation is the motor boat, usually called a "scow." It is approximately twenty feet long, four feet wide, and one foot deep. It is a flat-bottomed boat, draws very little water, and can carry heavy loads. The motor, or "kicker," is usually between ten and twenty horsepower.

During freeze-up (October 1 to November 1) long-distance transportation is sometimes undertaken using a combination of motorboat and dog team. The motorboat, loaded with dogs and sled, is used until the river ice solidifies, at which point the boat is abandoned and the trip is continued by dog team. In winter (November to mid-March) the major method of transportation is the dog team. The usual team consists of between four and six dogs, harnessed in single file. They pull a canvas-backed wood sled often called a "cariole." Although some men own snowmobiles, these are used mainly for trips between settlements or around town. Extended trips to the bush are always made by dog team.

During break-up (April 1 to May 15) the above methods – scow, snowmobile, and dog team – are not practicable. Therefore, only short journeys on foot are undertaken.

Air travel is used to reach hospitals, government centres, or job sites in distant locations. Aircraft are not chartered for private purposes, such as going to the trapline.

Fuel

Three basic kinds of fuel are used: electricity, gas, and wood. Electricity is used mainly for lighting, but most homes also have a few electric-powered items such as radios or record players. A government diesel engine generates the 117v AC electric power, the charge for which is calculated by the kilowatt hour. Battery electric power can be purchased from the Bay store and batteries are used to run most radio equipment. Gasoline and oil, also purchased locally from the Bay store, are used to run snowmobiles and "kickers" for the motorboats. Wood is used for heating and cooking and is obtained from the timberlands around Pe Tsʼéh Kı̨́. It is hauled to the house by snowmobile or dog team in the winter. The little additional wood that is required in the summer is usually hauled by government trucks. Goods which are not essential to the upkeep of the household include such things as: leather cowboy boots for the young men and stylish clothes for the young girls, a snowmobile, an extra or more powerful motor for the motorboat, a washing machine, a radio, or a record player. Aside from the washing machine these goods are generally purchased by and for the young unmarried adults. Cigarettes are also purchased by adults when extra money is available.

Map 2.1 Traditional Land Use Trails

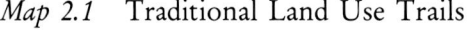

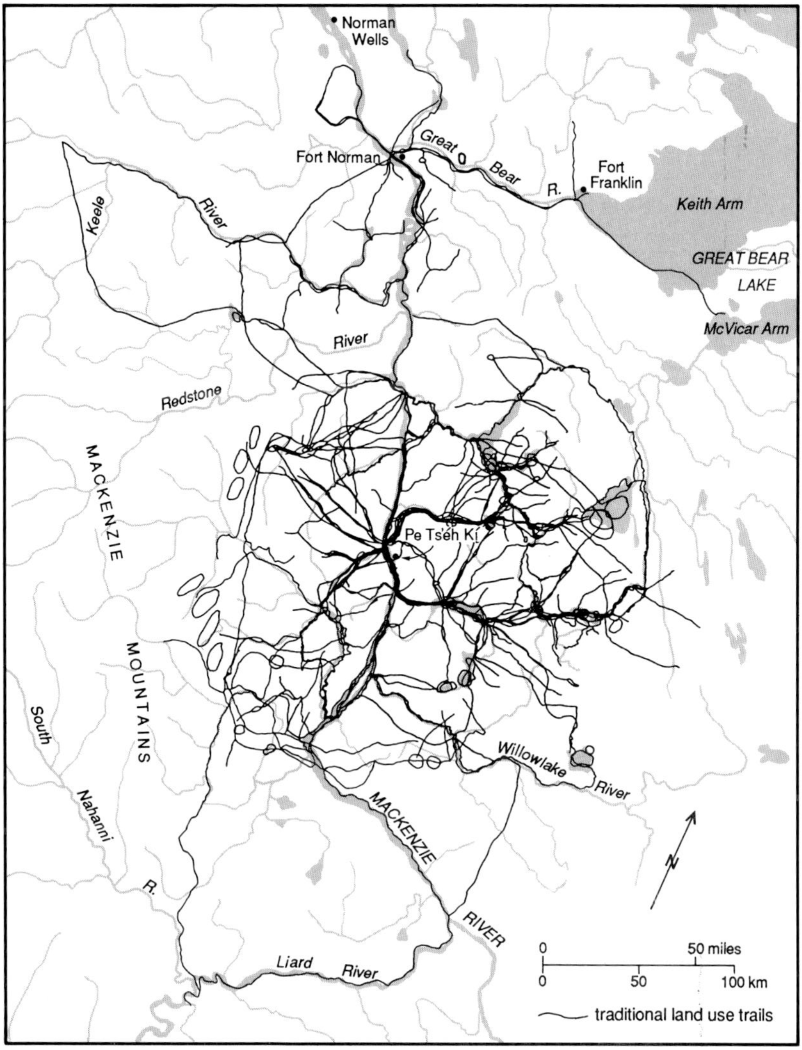

Material Resources and their Acquisition

They never stayed in one place. They moved all over the place, Blackwater Lake, Keller Lake, Birch Bark Lake. Hunting was more popular. People hunted for big game more than anything else including trapping.

Sometimes people came into town for supplies but in those days there were only two sicknesses: the cold and the sore stomach. Sometimes people hardly eat anything for two days, just drink water. It must make them sick.

Hudsons Bay used to be a strong outfit then, but they had to use spruce bark for the roof of their warehouse. The man who ran the store got people to get the spruce bark. Two men would have to carry one. It was very heavy. A pole with two men one at each end on a log to carry it up the hill. He helped them put on the spruce bark roof. He worked twenty days and earned forty dollars and he thought that was good money.

In the olden days no one knew anything about shipping furs out. It was very seldom that you'd see white people around down this way. In them days a marten was fifty cents.... Big male bear you get around forty dollars for a skin. Big beaver was three dollars. People would go after what had a good price: wolverine, wolf, otter, fox. If the price is not high, well nobody hunts them.

The price of beaver went up to four dollars. Marten went up to two dollars and fifty cents. The price wasn't bad after Easter until the First World War. The price of marten then was up to seven dollars and fifty cents. The price was good then, so people used to go out and trap. Some would get 40, 50, 60, or more. The limit was about 60.

Translation by E.H., July 6, 1970

In order for the Dene to fulfill the material requirements of daily life, each household must obtain both cash and bush resources. With respect to bush resources, the typical household must obtain at least

Drying meat

one moose, a few beaver, and a regular supply of other bush food each year. Government statistics show that in 1968-69 the Pe Tsʼéh Kį́ community as a whole produced 27,062 pounds of country food, excluding rabbits and fish (Economic Staff Group et al. 1973:63, 96, 107, 108). This is approximately 225 pounds per capita or (using fourteen households as the base number) 1,933 pounds of country food per household. To this figure should be added approximately 75 pounds per capita for fish and rabbits, making an average per household food production of approximately 2,775 pounds. Among the species harvested were forty-seven moose and ten caribou (*Ibid.*). This approximates the estimate obtained during the fieldwork in 1969-70.

Bush resources are obtained in the following ways. Birds are hunted with a .22 caliber rifle, while moose, caribou, bear, and other big game are taken with a high-powered rifle such as a .308. Rabbits and other small game used for food may be hunted with a .22 but are usually snared along rabbit trails. Fish are netted rather than caught with a hook and line. Different kinds of fish are obtained by using different sized openings in the fish net. In winter, nets are set under the ice at fish lakes; in summer, they are placed at quiet points near the shore of the Mackenzie River.

Berries, roots, and other plant life are collected by gathering from the wild. There is no cultivation. Firewood is obtained from stands surrounding Pe Tsʼéh Kį́ and is usually cut with a power saw, then hauled in winter by sled. A majority of the water comes from the government well and is delivered to each house twice a week. In addition, buckets are used to trap rainwater and often ice is hauled from the Mackenzie in winter.

The typical family requires at minimum $1000.00 per annum to fulfill consumer needs and to acquire and replace the capital goods which make possible the acquisition of bush resources. Capital goods include such items as tents, traps, rifles, shells, canoes, kickers, dog teams, and dogs. The cost of this productive technology can be estimated in several ways. Bisset (1967:357), when using Bodden (1981:114) to estimate the life expectancy of various items, calculated the cost of outfitting in 1966 as approximately $430 per outfit, exclusive of shells, sleeping bags, saws, and cooking gear. Bodden, ten years later, estimated the complete cost of an outfit (excluding snowmobile) at $814. The Regional Impact of a Northern Gas Pipeline Study (Economic Staff Group et al. 1973:30) estimated the cost of production to be 14-16 cents per pound, given an estimate of 38,852 pounds of meat within the community or 2,775 pounds per household, or over 300 pounds per capita. At 15 cents a pound this works out to $5,827.80 for the community, or $416.27 for each household. On balance, therefore, a reasonable estimate of costs would be between $400 and $600 per household per annum.

Necessary cash can be obtained in three ways: wage labour, piecework, and government allowance. Wage labour consists of full-time employment or casual labour in Pe Tséh Kį́, seasonal labour in the Mackenzie area, or full-time employment in Fort Simpson. The kinds of work available and estimated rates of pay are provided in Table 2.2 below.

Table 2.2 Wage Labour Positions and Earnings

Position	Earnings per Annum	# of Persons
1. Full-time Employment in Pe Tséh Kį́		
School Janitor	c. $6000	1
Airport Worker	c. $6000	1
H.B. Co. Clerk	c. $2000	1
2. Casual Employment in Pe Tséh Kį́		
Odd Jobs Such as Painting, Cleaning, etc.	$300-$1000	60
Babysitting	c. $50	5
3. Seasonal Labour		
Oil-rig Work	c. $3000	10
Barge-work - Cook	c. $4000	1
4. Full-time Employment in Fort Simpson		
Nurse's Aide	c. $2500*	2
Garage Attendant	c. $1000	1

*Probable wage is $50 per week. No one remained a full year.

Another source of income is piecework labour. This includes trapping fur-bearing animals to sell to the Bay store, or at an outside auction, and the making of handicrafts which are sold to the government handicraft office in Fort Simpson. The kinds of furs and their estimated cash value are provided in Table 2.3 below, while the kinds of handicrafts and their cash value can found in Table 2.4.

All handicrafts except canoes are produced by women. The average income from handicrafts is approximately $200, with a range from

$50 to $700. As the capital costs of producing handicrafts are minimal, it is (if we ignore labour time) a highly profitable undertaking which, for some households, forms an important source of family income, while for others it provides cash to purchase luxury items.

Table 2.3 Trapping

Animal	Season	Auction Price*	Frequency**
mink	Nov.-Feb.	$11.00	2
otter	Nov.-Apr.	$30.00	3
marten	Nov.-Feb.	$ 4.00	1
lynx	Nov.-Apr.	$25.00	2
wolverine	Nov.-Apr.	$40.00	3
muskrat	Nov.-Mar.	$ 0.75	1
beaver	Nov.-Mar.	$12.00	1
wolf***	Nov.-Apr.	$15.00	3
squirrel	Nov.-Apr.	$ 0.25	1
fox	Nov.-Apr.	$10.00	3

*Per pelt, at the Bay store in Pe Tšéh Kį.
**1 = frequent; 2 = supplemental; 3 = rare
***There is a $40 bounty on wolves. Therefore they are never sold for fur.

Table 2.4 Handicrafts

Items	Price Paid
moccasins (for women)	$ 8.00
moccasins (for men)	$10.00
mukluks	$35.00
vests	$35.00
toy canoes (made of wood)	$10.00

Trapping, in this instance also considered piecework, is done by men only, working in groups or as individuals. The average household income from trapping was approximately $500, with a range of between $200 and $1,200. Most households averaged between $400 and $800. These estimates are confirmed by government statistics (Economic Staff Group et al. 1973), which indicate that gross fur income in the Pe Tsʼéh Kį́ community in 1969-70 was $7,904.90. This figure works out to be an average of $564.64 per household. The same publication indicates that in the previous season 699 marten, 650 muskrat, 219 beaver, 45 mink and 44 lynx were taken. In short, for the typical household, the exchange value of trapping production roughly approximates the capital cost of harvesting all bush resources. As a consequence, it can be seen that the primary function of trapping for most families lies in the collection of food and other bush resources for their own consumption. The cash income generated through trapping is used to cover the expenses incurred in harvesting these resources.

Table 2.5 Government Allowance

Type of Allowance	Amount per Annum	# of Persons
Old age pension	$1000-$2000	5
Disability pension	$1200	1
Family allowance*	$200-$700	11 (families)
Welfare**	$200-$500	2

*Family allowance or "baby bonus" money is distributed monthly by the Government of Canada to all families with minor dependent children. The amount given to each family depends upon the number and ages of the children. This allowance is not considered by the general Canadian public, the Dene of Pe Tsʼéh Kį́, or the government to be a form of welfare.
**Including aid to unwed mothers.

Government allowances provide the third source of cash. There are four kinds of government allowance in Pe Tsʼéh Kį́: old age pension, disability pension, family allowance, and welfare. The funds from these sources are tabulated above in Table 2.5. It should be noted that welfare plays a minor role as a source of capital income in Pe Tsʼéh Kį́. The two families which receive welfare payments from time to time have many young children and not enough unmarried adult males to provide adequate income.

The Division of Labour

In order to provide an adequate cash and bush income each household divides its responsibilities. This division is structured primarily along gender and age lines.

The men are responsible mainly for the provision of cash resources; the collection of moose, caribou, fish, wood, and water; and the maintenance of the equipment used for taking their resources, as well as transportation gear. In the typical household there are at least two adult males. The senior male (i.e., the father) is usually responsible for providing a regular cash income. Usually this is achieved through full-time employment, old age pension, or disability allowance. A junior adult male (i.e., an unmarried son), often in his twenties, is mainly responsible for the provision of big game, fish, wood, water, and equipment maintenance. He will also contribute some cash income through trapping.

The adult women are mainly responsible for the provision of rabbits, birds, and berries, and for the maintenance of the household. Specifically, these latter duties include, among other tasks, food preparation, the repair and washing of clothes, tanning moose and caribou hide, making footwear and gloves for the family, and keeping the house in order. They may also contribute to the capital income of the household through the making and selling of handicrafts. In the typical household where there are at least two adult women these tasks are generally shared equally by the senior and the junior females.

Sewing a slipper

A typical family has four dependent children who share in the responsibility for obtaining berries and small game. They also cooperate in the performance of many household maintenance duties. By their presence, they ensure a regular source of cash income through the family allowance payments.

Ownership

All necessary material goods, including the house, stove, and furniture, belong to the household as a whole but are controlled by the adult women. Luxury items are owned by individuals, usually unmarried persons. The trapping and transportation equipment is owned by the household but controlled by the men. Bush houses are controlled by individual males but may be used by any relative. Property such as a lakeside trapping area may be controlled by an individual man, a group of brothers, or the males of related families. Any person may use the property, though in practice the right of exclusive control over a fish lake is respected (for further discussion see Chapter 3).

Bush resources are considered to belong primarily to the person and/or household that harvested them. It is nonetheless considered improper for an individual or a single household to keep for itself any bush resources (including such major food resources as moose meat) or indeed any food, whether from the bush or from the store. It is rather considered appropriate for these resources to be shared throughout the community. Exceptions to this do occur; however, even though a refrigerated locker was built by the Government of the Northwest Territories to store game meat, and people on occasion quietly acquire a horde of store bought items from, for example, camp sites abandoned by geologists, such exceptions are quite rare. Furs are considered to belong to the individual and/or the household which trapped them. Cash, as well, is controlled by the individual and/or household that earned it. However, once converted into food or some other useful item, the produce is considered to be part of the sharing system. In other words, sharing on the basis of reciprocity forms the backbone of the attitude towards ownership of all useful goods among the Pe Tséh Kį́ people.

Inheritance

When community members die their personal property is abandoned or burned. Real property such as lakeside trapping areas, in the control of the deceased person, apparently returns to the community as a whole, with the additional proviso, reinforced by religious sanctions, that the family should not make use of it again in the immediate future. It is said that when a man dies his soul inhabits his fish lake, and so it will be dangerous for the widow and her children to return. Therefore it is always recommended that a dead man's fish lake be abandoned by his family. However, there are no community sanctions against individuals or households that do not follow this rule and, like many other rules, there are some people who see them as applicable to their situation, and others who do not.

The Cycle of Daily Life

On a typical day adults generally arise between 6:00 a.m. and 7:00 a.m. The first to arise, usually the father, builds the fire in the cookstove and, in the winter, also in the heat stove. He or another adult then prepares the breakfast which will usually consist of tea and porridge or some prepared food.

Meals are taken two or three times a day, depending mainly upon the availability of food and the season. Although meals are often eaten piecemeal and there is no set schedule for mealtimes, generally speaking, the first meal is taken between 6:00 a.m. and 10:00 a.m., the afternoon meal, if any, between 12:00 noon and 2:00 p.m., and the evening meal between 5:00 p.m. and 8:00 p.m. Children may snack on bannock or store-bought candies throughout the day.

At some point during each day, firewood is taken from the storage area, chopped, and put in the wood box in the house. About once a week an adult male will go to the bush to cut and haul more wood for the house. Each day one or more members of the family will go to the Bay store to purchase goods and to gossip.

About three times a week the women will visit their snare lines and hunt for small game and birds. This is usually done in the late morning or early afternoon, but those who are considered to be the best providers will go early in the morning right after breakfast.

In the winter one or more of the adult males is away trapping and hunting for periods of between one and two weeks, while those at home take up some of the responsibilities for providing wood and maintaining gear. In the summer one or more adult males will go daily to visit the fish nets in the Mackenzie. The men feed the dogs daily in winter and fairly regularly in summer.

Visiting may take place at any time of the day. However, most often it occurs in the late afternoon or early evening. Often, especially in town in the winter, the men will play cards long into the night. Bedtime is between 9:00 p.m. and midnight; however, the actual time one goes to bed is decided by the individual, and a person may even go to sleep in the midst of household activities. Children tend to go to bed when it gets dark; this means that they are up much later in summer than in winter. Sleeping arrangements usually have the husband, wife, and baby, if any, in the largest bedroom, the daughter(s) in the middle bedroom, and the son(s) in the front bedroom. Some of the adult sons may sleep in the living shack behind the house.

This routine holds true throughout the year, especially in the winter. In the summer, however, whole households may leave Pe Tsʼéh Kį́ for periods of between a week and two months, either to visit relations in Fort Norman, Fort Franklin, or Fort Simpson, or to live in the bush. When this occurs, the house is locked and the windows are bolted. On occasion, during the summer, less than one-half of the Pe Tsʼéh Kį́ households may be in town.

Individual Knowledge and Economic Activities

The wide range of economic activities pursued by each household requires persons who have knowledge of the bush, wage employment, the workings of machinery and government programs. Knowledge for working in the latter three comes both from direct experience and, largely, through training courses or instructions from government personnel.

Knowledge of the bush and in particular the skills needed to hunt, trap and process materials effectively are derived in the first place through direct experience with knowledgable persons, often elders. One learns primarily by watching and doing; there is little verbal transmission of information, especially out of context. Of great importance both to practical matters and to building self-confidence, is knowledge learned through entering relationships with the spirit world of the animals. Hunters are expected to have contact with this spirit world through a special relationship with one species of animal. This relationship is signalled by a taboo on eating the flesh of any representatives of the species. Sometimes the relationship is explained as being with the species as a whole. At others, it is seen as pertaining to a particular animal (called a "medicine animal"). Predicting events through a form of "dreaming true" that connects people to the spirit world provides an additional means whereby some individuals learn about matters that relate to the bush (as well as matters that range far beyond hunting). "Dreaming true" is something not all Slavey Dene are able to do. Once one possesses it, if used properly, it seems to be a skill that can be improved over time, so that elders are more frequently able to actually "dream true" and are able to do so over a wider range of subjects. Through direct experience, entering relations with medicine animals and "dreaming true," hunters in each household are able to predict with a good degree of certainty the location and behaviour of species of animals in general as well as, on occasion, the particular place and time a specific animal's trail will intersect with that of a hunter.

Economic Variation Among Households

All fourteen households meet their economic needs successfully. Of the fourteen households, eight can be said to have had little difficulty in attaining this goal. Five of these are what may be called typical households. In these cases cash for the household is obtained by the senior couple, generally through old age pensions with supplements through family allowance payments. The unmarried adult son or sons are responsible for providing labour for the production of major bush resources, as well as some income through trapping. They do this by going to the bush either by themselves or with unmarried men from kin-related households. The unmarried adult daughters, along with their mother, provide labour for processing bush resources and for collecting small game and berries. Usually cash earned by the sons through wage labour, such as oil-rig work, or by the daughters through handicrafts or wage labour belongs to them personally and is used to purchase luxury items. The sixth household is exactly the same except that it contains no dependent children. In the seventh household the father has a permanent job, his adult sons collect bush resources and, although there are no adult daughters, his wife is able to share her collecting and processing activities by working with her sisters and her younger daughters. In the eighth household the roles are somewhat reversed in that one adult son has a good seasonal job as a cook and contributes part of his income to the household coffers. In this household bush resources are collected primarily by the father, rather than his sons.

Six Pe Tsʼéh Kį́ households have difficulties maintaining themselves as independent economic units. The stress they experience arises either from difficulty in obtaining sufficient cash or sufficient labour power to fulfill their economic needs or both. The most common problem (five of the six) is that there is no guaranteed source of cash income, because no one has a permanent job or steady work, and the senior couple is too young for old age pension. As the wife in one of these households put it, "when my husband reaches sixty [the following year], then we'll be in the money." In each of these households the senior male participates by hunting and trapping. However, unlike the typical families, here the objective of obtaining furs to generate surplus cash becomes a primary rather than a secondary focus of the bush activities. In three cases sufficient income is generated by trapping, supplemented by family allowance and, occasionally by welfare (although this was rather minimal), to easily maintain self-sufficiency. Here the stress caused by the lack of a guaranteed source of income is not overwhelming, but, given the depressed nature of the fur market, these households suffer from a significant degree of economic insecurity. A further complication for some families (including two of these three) is the lack of adult sons to provide labour for trapping. This means that the senior males, some of whom were in their late fifties, have to work extremely hard to provide sufficient cash and bush resource needs when hunting and trapping.

For the last two of the households without a guaranteed cash income, difficulties arise because the males cannot provide sufficient cash and country food from the bush. In both cases this is due to insufficient labour power to provide for the family's need. In one case there is a young and rather large family and therefore insufficient labour to provide for these needs. These families have a chronic problem in both sectors and tend to rely on welfare to supplement family allowance payments and on cash borrowed from close kin and the benefits of the sharing system that exists in the bush sector in order to maintain their economic autonomy.

For one household the stress occurs in the bush sector. Here the father is young and has a full-time job. His household consists only of younger children, which means that, unlike the other Dene male with a full-time job, he has no unmarried adult sons to provide bush income. As a result he tends to spend many of his free evenings and weekends on the land in an attempt to provide for his bush sector needs. He must generally do this work alone because his full-time job imposes a different schedule from the other men.

As the above indicates, all Pe Tséh Kį́ households are able to adapt, with differing degrees of stress, to an economic orientation that has developed since the move into town. However, it can also be seen that the most successful adjustment has been made by those households that have sufficient members to cover all the needs. These households tend to be mature in the sense that they consist of an older couple and unmarried adult children. The least successful adaptations are made by those who have insufficient labour power, that is, the senior male has no assistance in the bush sector. Therefore, in Pe Tséh Kį́ it is just barely economically feasible to begin a new household, even if one has a full-time permanent job. This provides a significant impediment to marriage and the establishment of new households. Hence, the specific economic adaptation, while successful in the short run, discourages the actions necessary to achieve the long-term objective — the successful reproduction of the social system as a whole.

Footnotes

1. Two widows also have permanent houses in town. However, these individuals do not constitute independent households.

2. The other house was built by an Indian. It is made of sideboard with shingles and is approximately 23' x 36'. It is presently unoccupied and therefore I never saw the interior.

Chapter Three

Social Structure and Organization

Summary of Kinship System

Historically, the fundamental unit of Pe Tsʼéh Kį́ social organization was the local band, a group of roughly twenty to thirty kin-related individuals who resided for most of the winter at a particular fish lake. In addition there was a regional band, composed of three local bands, which served effectively as the marriage isolate for the Pe Tsʼéh Kį́ people. After the move into the town of Pe Tsʼéh Kį́, three significant social units emerged: the household; households of certain closely related kin — a group that corresponds closely with the local bands that existed when the Pe Tsʼéh Kį́ people lived in the bush; and the community, which corresponds closely to the regional band that existed previously.

When people lived in the bush interaction was focussed primarily on the individual household and those kin-related households with which one camped. For most of the year there was little interaction with, or even proximity to, households or local bands with which one did not camp. The entire regional band only gathered together on special occasions such as festive events and holidays, usually in the town. There was a strong tendency to marry people who were outside of one's own local band, but within the grouping of local bands that formed the regional band.

The move into town brought two important changes. First and foremost, households which would not have been part of the local band in the bush were now neighbours. This, plus the increase in the number of people with whom one resided (from approximately 30 to 120), caused friction that did not exist when people lived in the bush. Second, the grouping of people from which marriage partners were selected in the past now lived in the same community. This created a significant problem because it had not been appropriate for people who reside together to marry.

These two difficulties had an important impact on the social dynamics of the community. The immediate effect could be described as a lack of social solidarity within the community. One solution was to declare, through kinship manipulation, that the community was the equivalent of a large local band. This solution worked well for two of the bands (labelled B in the text) which, in effect, amalgamated into one. However, it only worked partially to incorporate the third band (labelled A1 and A2 in the text). In practice, the community would see itself as composed of two bands that were not closely related and should not be residing together. However, in its ideology, members of the community would often express that Pe Tséh Kį́ was like a single local band: a view confirmed at events such as the Drum Dance where the sense of social solidarity associated with that sentiment were realized. But such sentiments had a cost. Since the traditional marriage norms did not sanction intermarriage between co-residents, the creation of a single local band out of what once was the marriage isolate, in order to produce social solidarity in the present, created a long-term difficulty. It reduced, and indeed came close to eliminating, the possibility of intermarriage among the Pe Tséh Kį́ people. In other words, this solution severely curtailed the potential for the reproduction of the Pe Tséh Kį́ society. The alternative solution, to permit intermarriage between the two groups and hence create social solidarity through "alliance" did not occur. As a result, relations between the two groups were in unresolved dynamic tension.

This social dynamic became apparent in the first place through a novel interpretation of literature on the northern Dene and their kinship terminology. For this reason it is not put forward as the only correct interpretation. The standard interpretation is based on what is called Mackenzie Basin Type terminology, which, reinforced by their own experiences, has convinced many researchers that the basic unit of social organization of a community like Pe Tséh Kį́ is the "nodal kindred," i.e., a grouping of households linked by close biological kin ties, usually to a particular elder individual or couple. In this interpretation Pe Tséh Kį́ would be perceived as consisting of approximately three or four such units, each co-existing in some harmony with the others.

I am suggesting that the terminology used in Pe Tséh Kį́ really implies a Dravidianate system. Here the social world would be conceptualized as consisting of two primary groups: "kinsmen" or those with whom one could co-reside without intermarriage and "allies" or those with whom one could co-reside only after marriage. In this view, Pe Tséh Kį was attempting to resolve its new circumstances by transforming bands that had been allies in the pre-town period into kinsmen. This was successful with respect to the two groups labelled B, but only partially successful between them and the group labelled A. Without the use of intermarriage or the ability to completely transform the kinship, neither of the traditional means to create social solidarity among co-residents could be used.

At the end of this chapter two suggestions are made concerning the resolution of this problem. The first is that the use of nodal kindreds may be a response, especially by younger members of the Dene community, to the difficulties created by the "Dravidianate" situation in the contemporary period. The second suggestion is that the Pe Tséh Kį Dene have developed a notion of kinship which parallels the Euro-Canadian system. This is described in the anthropological literature as Eskimoan terminology because some Inuit societies employ kinship terms which are similiar to those of Euro-Canadians. An implication of the idea that the kinship system of the Slavey Dene conforms to the Dravidian type for Lévi-Strauss's theory of kinship structures as expounded in *The Elementary Structures of Kinship* appears as Appendix D in this text.

The Kinship Terminology

The kinship terminological system described by Helm (1961:55) at Lynx Point conforms to the "Mackenzie Basin Type" as described by Spier (1925:76f). In this system the first ascending and first descending generations follow the pattern of the "Dravidian" system, while those in ego's generation follow the generational pattern that is usually described as "Hawaiian." In other words the key to a Mackenzie Basin terminology as described by Spier is that ego differentiates between cross and parallel relatives in the two adjacent generations but does not make that distinction for his own.

At Pe Tséh Kį most individuals use terminology consistent with the Mackenzie Basin terminological system described by Helm for Lynx Point. However, this pattern may represent a transformation of an underlying Dravidianate system. In this latter system cross and parallel relations are expressed in all generations including ego's, and the same cross term is utilized to designate both consanguines, such as mother's brother, and affines, such as father-in-law, who belong to the same generation and are of the same sex (Dumont 1953:35). Following this logic Dravidianate systems, in Dumont's view, create structural oppositions between kinsmen, or those who belong to one's own side, and affines, or those who belong to the other side (*Ibid.*: 39). In this system marriage is structurally possible between persons of the same generation who are defined as affines to each other, but is impossible among those who are defined as kinsmen. It is suggested here that Pe Tséh Kı́ kinship terminology is Dravidianate, and its band organization gives some indication of the structural oppositions described by Dumont.

The choice of parallel terms to indicate cross-cousins arises in the everyday speech of the Pe Tséh Kı́ people for two important reasons. First, there is a strong ideological commitment to discourage intermarriage among members of the same local band; that is, there is a strong sentiment toward band exogamy. Given the possibility that a brother and sister could both be members of the same band as married adults, and that they could each have children who would in principle be marriageable under a strict application of the Dravidian rules, a terminological transformation to discourage this possibility occurs. Second, intermarriage among biological first cross-cousins is discouraged, presumably regardless of where they reside. As a result of both of these tendencies, the cross-cousin term for such cases is routinely transformed into a parallel one, thus changing potential affines into kinsmen; hence, the apparent creation of a Mackenzie Basin terminological type among the Pe Tséh Kı́ Dene.

Most people in Pe Tséh Kı́ will respond to queries about the kinship system by using Mackenzie Basin terms. The possibility that a Dravidianate system underlies it was only revealed after intensive work with a few individuals and, in particular, with a woman who was completely fluent in Slavey and English and who had a thorough knowledge both of the logic of the kinship system and of the set of actual kin relations for virtually all Dene living in Pe Tséh Kı́, Fort Norman, Fort Simpson, and Fort Providence over at least four generations. The kinship discussion that follows relies on this analysis rather than one based on Mackenzie Basin terms and so adds a dimension to the description of kin terms provided by Helm for Lynx Point.

The kinship terminological system of Pe Tséh Kı́ follows the classic Dravidianate pattern. Thus, for example, as the tables below indicate, parallels in the first descending generations are considered to be children of either same sex parallels or opposite sex cross relatives, while crosses are those children of either sex parallels or same sex cross relatives (*Ibid.*: 36). In the second ascending and descending generations the cross-parallel dichotomy is not used. All persons of the second descending generation are given the same generational term regardless of their sex, while a simple male-female dichotomy is used in the second ascending generation. It is interesting to note that, for affines, the spouse's siblings are considered as cross, while the siblings' spouses are parallels. The same opposite holds for the spouses of siblings. This pattern can be extended indefinitely and allows for the development of a wide set of lateral ties. The parents of a spouse are given a cross designation, while in the first descending generation, the system uses the very cross-parallel and same sex-opposite sex contrasts found for consanguines. In short, the kinship terminology follows a Dravidianate system.

Figure 3.1 Consanguines – Male Ego

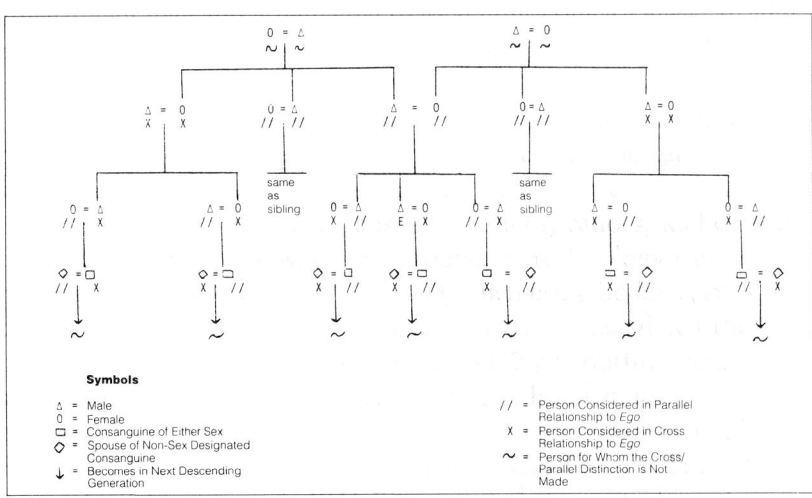

Figure 3.2 Consanguines — Female Ego

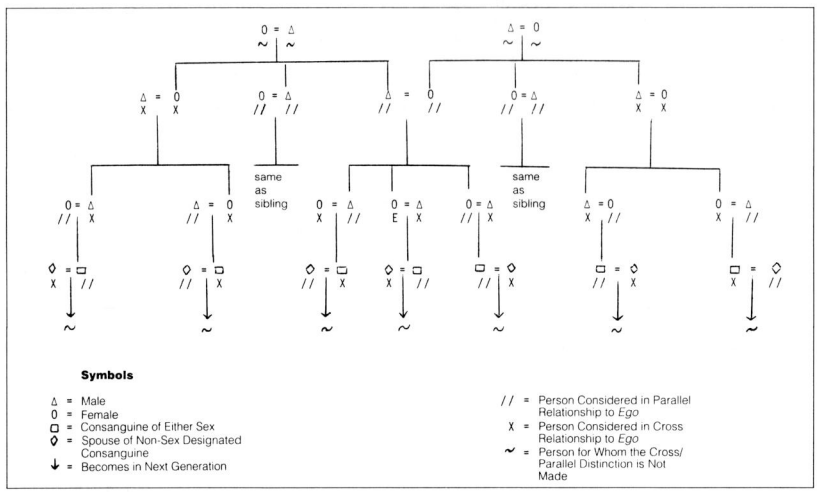

Figure 3.3 Affines — Male Ego

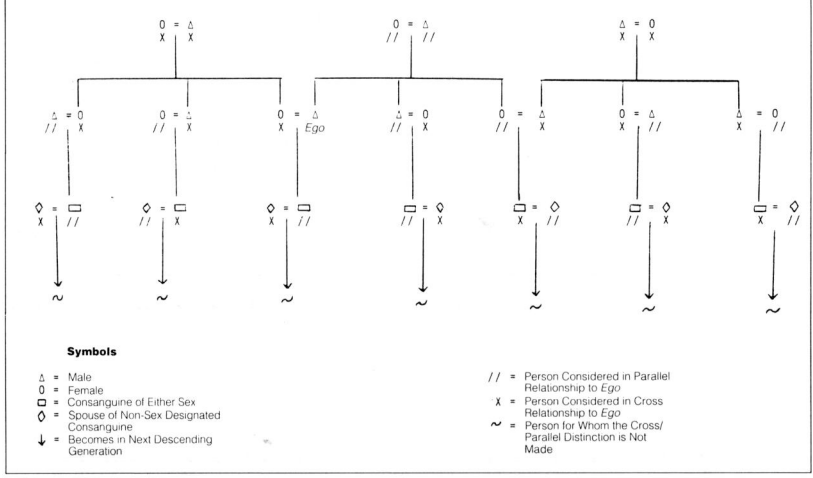

Figure 3.4 Affines — Female Ego

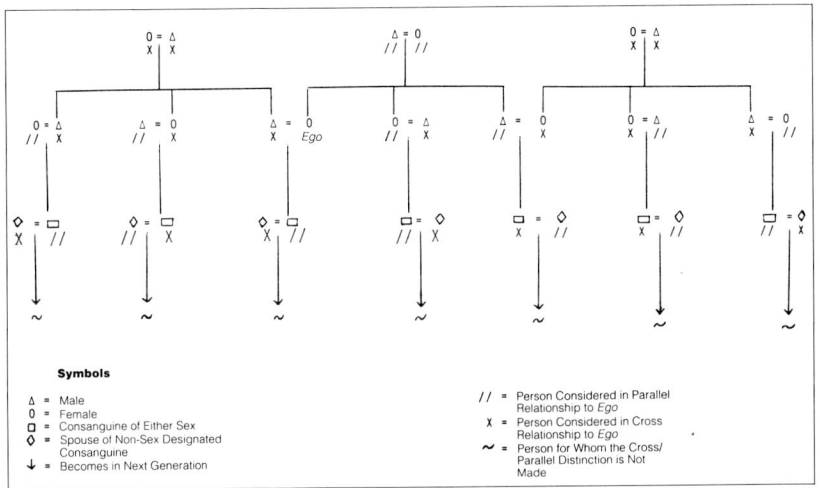

Definitions of the Slavey Kinterms

ehtsée: "Old man," "Grandfather":[1] Any male of the +2 generation; any older man. Refers usually to FaFa and MoFa.

ehtsį: "Old woman," "Grandmother": A female of the +2 generation; any elderly woman. Refers usually to FaMo and MoMo.

setá: "Father": Ego's biological father or his mother's husband. The term applies only to Fa. It is derived from the root *-ta* (FaBr) to which the prefix *se* (my own) has been added. Compare *gotáa*.

semo: "Mother": Ego's biological mother or his father's wife. The term applies only to Mo. It is derived from the root *-mo* (MoSi) to which the prefix *se* (my own) has been added. Compare *empo*.

gotáa: "Uncle": (1) Ego's father's brother. (2) Any male of the +1 generation who stands in a parallel cousin relationship to ego's father.[2] The term generally refers to FaBr, MoSiHu. It is derived from *ehtáa* (father's brother) to which the prefix go meaning "one's" has been added. The term is of local usage only. Other Slaveys use *ehtáa* to indicate the relationship.

emǫ́: "Auntie": (1) Ego's mother's sister. (2) Any female of the +1 generation who stands in a parallel cousin relationship with ego's mother. Refers usually to MoSi and FaBrWi.

seʔeh: "Uncle," "Inlaw," "Father in law": (1) Ego's mother's brother. (2) Any male of the +1 generation who stands in a cross-cousin relationship with ego's father.³ (3) Spouse's father and any male who is in a parallel relationship with him. Refers specifically to MoBr, FaSiHu, spouse's Fa.

ehmbée: "Auntie," "Inlaw," "Mother in law": (1) Ego's father's sister. (2) Any female of the +1 generation who stands in a cross-cousin relationship with ego's mother. (3) Spouse's mother and any female who is in a parallel cousin relationship with her. Refers most frequently to FaSi, MoBrWi, and spouse's Mo.

sį: "I": Refers exclusively to ego.

goįnde: "Brother," "Cousin": (1) Ego's older brother. (2) Any older male of the 0 generation who is in a parallel cousin relationship with ego. Refers most commonly to ego's older Br, FaBrSo, MoSiSo. Also used for FaSiDaHu, MoBrDaHu.

sechia: "Little brother," "Cousin": (1) Ego's younger brother. (2) Any younger male of the 0 generation who stands in a parallel cousin relationship with ego. Refers most commonly to ego's younger Br, FaBrSo, MoSiSo. Also used for FaSiDaHu, MoBrDaHu.

sechia (2):
Female Ego Only: (sometimes) "Nephew": (1) Ego's brother's son. (2) Any younger male of the -1 generation whose father stands in a parallel cousin relationship with ego. (3) Ego's daughter's husband. Term is used most frequently in reference to BrSo, FaSiDaSo, MoBrDaSo,

FaBrSoSo, MoSiSoSo, DaHu. (Note: The use of this term is consonant with the use of parallel terms only to designate cousin. Also see *sebaa* (2) and *sedo*.)

sembae: "Sister," "Cousin": (1) Ego's older sister. (2) Any older female of the 0 generation who is in a parallel cousin relationship to ego. Refers most commonly to ego's older Si, FaBrDa, MoSiDa. Also refers to FaSiSoWi, MoBrSoWi.

sedea: "Sister," "cousin": (1) Ego's younger sister. (2) Any younger female of the 0 generation who is in a parallel cousin relationship with ego. Refers most commonly to ego's younger Si, FaBrDa, MoSiDa. Also refers to FaSiSoWi, MoBrSoWi.

selah: "Inlaw," "Cousin": (1) Any individual of the 0 generation who stands in a cross-cousin relationship to ego regardless of sex. (2) Spouse's siblings and individuals who stand in a parallel cousin relationship to them. Refers most often to MoBrSo, MoBrDa, FaSiSo, FaSiDa; spouse's brothers and sisters; also MoSiSoWi, MoSiDaHu, etc. (Note: Some Pe Tsʼéh Kį́ people, as is the case at Lynx Point, commonly use parallel cousin terms for all cousins. For them *selah* is used for in-laws only.)

segheh: "Cousin (male)," "Brother-in-law": (1) Any male individual of the 0 generation who stands in a cross relation to ego. (2) Spouse's male siblings and individuals who stand in a parallel relationship to them. Refers most often to MoBrSo, FaSiSo, spouse's brothers.

sezhaa: "Son": (1) Ego's male child. Refers only to So.

sezhaa (2)
Male Ego Only: "Son": (1) Ego's brother's son. (2) Any male of the -1 generation whose father stands in a parallel cousin relationship to ego. Refers most commonly to BrSo, FaBrSoSo, MoSiSoSo, FaSiDaSo, MoBrDaSo.

sezhaa (3)
Female Ego Only:
"Son": (1) Ego's sister's son. (2) Any male of the -1 generation whose mother stands in a parallel cousin relationship to ego. (3) Ego's daughter's husband. Refers most commonly to SiSo, MoSiDaSo, FaBrDaSo, FaSiSoSo, MoBrSoSo. (Can be used for DaHu when cross-parallel opposition is to be avoided. This is very rare.)

setié:
"Daughter": Ego's female child. Refers only to Da.

setié (2)
Male Ego Only:
"Daughter": (1) Ego's brother's daughter. (2) Any female of the -1 generation whose father stands in a parallel cousin relationship to ego. Refers generally to BrDa, FaBrSoDa, MoSiSoDa, FaSiDaDa, MoBrDaDa.

setié (3)
Female Ego Only:
"Daughter": (1) Ego's sister's daughter. (2) Any female of the -1 generation whose mother stands in a parallel cousin relationship to ego. Refers usually to SiDa, MoSiDaDa, FaBrDaDa, FaSiSoDa, MoBrSoDa.

setié (4)
Female Ego Only
(archaic): "Son-in-law": Ego's daughter's husband. This term was in current usage for a short period of time about fifty years ago.

sebaa:
Male Ego Only:
"Nephew": (1) Ego's sister's son. (2) Any male of the -1 generation whose father stands in a cross-cousin relationship to ego. (3) Ego's daughter's husband. The term refers most commonly to SiSo, FaSiSoSo, MoBrSoSo, FaBrDaSo, MoSiDaSo, DaHu.

sebaa (2)
Female Ego Only:
"Nephew": (1) Ego's brother's son. (2) Any male of the -1 generation whose mother stands in a cross-cousin relationship to ego. The term most commonly refers to BrSo, MoBrDaSo, FaSiDaSo, MoSiSoSo, FaBrSoSo. (Note: This usage seems consonant with a system in which ego distinguishes terminologically between parallel and cross-cousins. Also see *sechia* and *sedo*.)

sendaa:
Male Ego Only:
"Niece": (1) Ego's sister's daughter. (2) Any female of the -1 generation whose father stands in a cross-cousin relationship with ego. (3) Ego's son's wife.

	Refers specifically to SiDa, FaSiSoDa, MoBrSoDa, FaBrDaDa. MoSiDaDa, SoWi. (Note: For female equivalent see *secháa*.)
secháa: *Female Ego Only*:	"Niece": (1) Ego's brother's daughter. (2) Any female of the -1 generation whose mother stands in a cross-cousin relationship to ego. (3) Ego's son's wife. (4) Ego's sister's son's wife. (5) The wife of any male of the -1 generation whose mother stands in a parallel cousin relationship to ego. Refers specifically to BrDa, FaBrSoDa, MoSiSoDa, SoWi, SiSiWi. (Note: The use of this term seems perhaps more consonant with the use of parallel terms to designate all cousins in ego's generation. As well, it skews generation, a factor which is unique in this terminology, except for its rare usage by males in similar circumstances. No female ego term equivalent to *sendaa* was found. This could be because of a research error or because it does not exist. If the latter is the case, then it would appear to function first as a means to inhibit marriage in this case and second as a means to create cross-parallel ambiguities that might prove useful in reckoning relations.)
secháa (2) *Female Ego Only*:	"Grandson," "Granddaughter": Any individual of the -2 generation. Refers specifically to ego's grandchildren through both parallel and cross-cousin relationships.
sepii:	*Male Ego Only*: "Grandson," "Granddaughter": Any individual of the -2 generation. Refers specifically to ego's grandchildren through both parallel and cross-cousin relationships.
sepii (2) *Male Ego Only*:	"?" (rare): Ego's daughter's husband.
sedené: *Female Ego Only*:	"My husband": Ego's husband. It is derived from *dene* (man).
sets'éke: *Male Ego Only*:	"My wife": Ego's wife. It is derived from *ts'éke* (woman).

sedo: "?" (1) Ego's daughter's husband. (2) The husband
Female Ego Only: of any female of the -1 generation whose mother stands in a parallel relationship to ego. Refers specifically to DaHu.

Tracing Kin Ties and Descent

For most people in Pe Tséh Kį́ the remembered genealogical record is shallow, going back in time only as far as the memory of the oldest living member of the community. Instead, relationships are traced through living persons, generally through lateral ties either in ego's generation or in the +1 generation.[4] Thus, two men who call each other "brother," and act accordingly, may be related only through distant lateral ties (such as one's mother's sister's husband's sister's son), rather than use an apparently obvious direct lineal relationship (such as in the case of a father's father's brother's son's son, where the men of the +2 generation are dead).

Nonetheless, while the system may be shallow lineally, individuals maintain an extensive lateral kinship record. Most adults living in Pe Tséh Kį́ can quote the lateral network of kinship ties which bind together the Slavey Dene of Fort Simpson, Jean Marie River, Pe Tséh Kį́, Fort Norman, and Fort Franklin; and when pressed, some are able to trace relationships to persons as far away as Fort Providence and Yellowknife to the south, and Fort Good Hope to the north. Some of these models, especially among the older women, rival in scope and completeness the lineal models maintained by individuals in other parts of the world.

Descent is bilateral and kinship ties are traced through living persons without reference to descent or the genealogical record. However, the descent principle is used to maintain the tie between same sex siblings after the death of both parents. It may also be used to establish a link between other individuals through a tie between their parents or other persons in the first ascending generation.

The kin terms are learned by copying the terms used by older siblings of the same sex. When this is not possible, a child will follow the terms used by the same sex parent. In this way the child will always produce the proper cross-parallel, male-female relationship, incorrect only as to generational tie. In some instances children may be told of certain kinship relationships and their terminological referents. This is done most often with regard to relationships with other children.

Social Relations Within the Household

The minimal unit of social organization within the community is the household. Normally this unit can be defined as a nuclear-extended family consisting of a father, mother, at least one adult son and daughter, and about four younger sons and daughters.

Relations between family members are structured along sex and age lines. The ties between same sex members are very close, while those between opposite sex members, including brother-sister and husband-wife, are distant and restrained. Leadership within each single sex group is asserted by the eldest individual present, with the younger invariably taking a dependent position. As described in Chapter 2, household activities are also governed by a sexual division. It is expected that older persons of each sex will tend to teach and discipline their younger, same sex counterparts.[5] The separation of the sexes breaks down only when the family travels together, but even here they remain segregated in their activities and interaction patterns.

The sexual division continues after the death of both parents and/or the formal breakup of the nuclear family unit. Ties between siblings of the same sex tend to remain strong, while those between siblings of the opposite sex seem to slowly disintegrate. This pattern is reflected in the relocation of individual family members after the dissolution of the natal nuclear family unit. Same sex siblings generally choose to live close to each other, while opposite sex siblings often settle far away from each other. In instances where family members of both sexes are married and live in Pe Tsʼéh Kı́, opposite sex siblings have moved to the opposite corners of the town; in instances where the siblings of only one sex are married and living in Pe Tsʼéh Kı́, siblings of the opposite sex have chosen to live elsewhere. The sexual division is echoed in the kinship terminological system which equates ego's children with those of his same sex siblings, while it distinguishes his children from his opposite sex siblings' children with a collateral designation.

Marriage Rules and Practice

Marriages between individuals who are not raised, or do not reside, in the same band, and who are not biologically close, are considered most desireable. Nevertheless, following a Dravidianate pattern, marriage between persons who are described as parallel cousins, regardless of their biological closeness, is considered improper, though it does happen occasionally. Further, while it is said that marriage between closely related cross-cousins or cross-cousins residing in one band is discouraged, it is not considered improper to the same extent as is the case with parallel cousins. However, it too occurred only rarely.

Positive sanction, then, is given only to marriages among persons not considered to be related; these are primarily individuals who are defined as cross-cousins with no tie through biology or residence. In support of a nodal kindred notion, some individuals consider that there could be people to whom they were unrelated in the Euro-Canadian sense; that is, Dene who were neither kinsmen nor allies to ego and with whom marriage would be considered proper.

M: Did brothers marry sisters? Not their own sisters. But if you married one sister would your brother marry the other sister?
T: Vice versa. You marry your brother-in-law's sister.
M: And he marries your sister?
T: Uh, huh. That was in line. Because you're not of the same blood.

Among the fourteen married couples in the community at the time of the fieldwork, thirteen were explainable in Dravidianate terms as cross-cousin marriages. Of these, only two were with close, biological cross-cousins. One marriage was between individuals socially perceived to be parallel cousins, although they were only distantly related biologically. While the marriage did occur, it was always remembered as an exception. Indeed, it was reported by some close kin from the husband's side that they would continue to call the wife "sister," even though they were not related by blood; they "were not going to change [just] because they got married" (Fieldnotes 20 March 1970). Such concerns are more consistent with a Dravidian orientation than the one typically utilized to describe Slavey band organization.

Residence after Marriage

Using the traditional ethnological categories, residence is bilocal. That is, after temporary matrilocality, the couple is free to reside with either the husband's or the wife's parents. No preference was stated, at least in these terms. It was only on rare occasions that a couple would choose not to reside in either parental band.

Obligations of the newly wedded couple to their in-laws are minimal. It is improper, however, for a son-in-law not to help out if his in-laws do not have adult sons and he is residing in his wife's community. Although the daughter-in-law does not have the same obligations, she may help the mother-in-law from time to time; this assistance is usually reciprocated by the mother-in-law.

Another dimension to post-marital residence, which seemed to shape behaviour, concerns the siblings of the couple more than the parents. Although little was said, an examination of Pe Tsʼéh Kį́ bands over the years reveals that they are formed by same sex siblings. It would appear from observation, as well as verbal description, that the ideal band would be a group of biological sisters married to a group of biological brothers. This suggests that bands are formed around cores of same-sex siblings rather than by descent through parents. In such a system a couple's decision regarding residence after marriage would be strongly influenced by the residence of each person's same sex siblings. Thus, a female partner would likely choose to live with her sister's band rather than her brother's, especially if her parents also reside in her sister's band. It may be assumed that a corresponding principle governs the male partner.

The Band Organization of Pe Tsʼéh Kı̨́: An Historical Note

The ancestors of the contemporary Pe Tsʼéh Kı̨́ community in the late 1800s comprised three primary bands each of which resided in the region to the east of the Mackenzie River somewhere between the present locales of Fort Simpson and Fort Norman. Another grouping of Pe Tsʼéh Kı̨́ people, the Mountain People, camped in the mountains to the west of the community. They left for the Yukon, it is reported, around the time of the Treaty signing in 1921. By the time the first trading post, later called Wrigley, was established in the late nineteenth century, the three bands had intermarried and appear to have created what might be termed a regional band (Helm 1965:375). Although many marriages were contracted outside the regional band, it remained the primary marriage isolate for the community that now resides at Pe Tsʼéh Kı̨́.

Over the span of seventy to eighty years between the formation of the regional band and their move into Pe Tsʼéh Kı̨́, there were at different times two or three local bands. Each of these bands would winter at different fish lakes. In the summer all would travel to Pe Tsʼéh Kı̨́. Occasionally, all of the bands wintered at a single lake. Over the period as a whole, however, two lake areas were predominantly used. One of these is nearer the community of Fort Simpson at the southern end of the regional band's land use and occupancy area; the other nearer Fort Norman at the northern end. When the regional band came to town a similar binary division emerged in their settlement pattern. Those that camped in winter in the south would camp at the northern end of the town, while those who camped in the north would dwell at the southern end. Between the bands that camped at each lake were the buildings constructed by non-natives (such as the Bay store and the Catholic church). In this period, the dwelling places of the Pe Tsʼéh Kı̨́ Dene, while in town, were stretched in a virtual single file along a north-south line and parallel to the bank of the Mackenzie River.

In the late 1950s and 1960s, the Government of Canada decided to encourage all native people, including the northern Dene, to abandon their traditional lifeways and to adopt a more mainstream Canadian one. To this end, they constructed new school facilities and other amenities in what were previously only summer camping grounds for many native people. Due to these apparently positive incentives and mechanisms that tied the input of necessary cash into the household economy to residence in town (see Asch 1977), Dene began to move into the regional towns. The Pe Tséh Kį́ Dene were no exception. In addition to the standard inducements to move out of the bush, the government promised to construct a new town of Pe Tséh Kį́ to be located on the east bank of the Mackenzie River some six miles south of the west bank locale described above. By 1966 the first house was ready for occupation.

In 1966, there were three local bands and a total population of 100 to 110. Two of the local bands camped at the southern lake, the other at the northern one. It would have been extremely interesting to discover how the autonomous bands might have chosen to co-reside in the new community, however, this is not possible. Since only one house could be built at a time, the government decided to place the first log cabin dwelling in the middle of the planned community, and gave it to one of the families which had camped at the northern end of the old Pe Tséh Kį́. The result of this manner of assigning housing priorities was to skew any rational decision-making based on choices related to band composition. Despite these conditions, some band organizational patterns emerged. One can only imagine how the autonomous bands, left to themselves, might have chosen to co-reside.

The Settlement Pattern of Pe Tséh Kį́

After the selection of houses was completed, the settlement pattern of the town followed the pattern illustrated in Map 3.5, dividing the community into three parts. The first, labelled B, is a central core consisting of six households. This part of the community represents those households in the two bands that lived at the southern lake and camped at the north end of the earlier Pe Tséh Kį́. The central core is flanked by two rows: A1 consists of three households, A2 consists of five. The groups labelled A represent those households who lived at the northern lake and camped at the southern end of the old Pe Tséh Kı́.

Following the depiction of the community contained in Map 1.2, Pe Tséh Kı́ appears to be laid out in a north-south orientation parallel to the bank of the Mackenzie River and along the main telecommunications line, called the CN line. An examination of the trails indicates, however, that the community orientation is toward the river as well as along it. The main set of foot routes leads from the westernmost row of houses toward the river. Once at the river bank, this system of trails combines to create three main routes down the bank toward the river. The trails indicate that each of the three groupings has created a separate trail system that allows access to the river without ever crossing the houses of any household not in their group.

Map 3.5   Kinship and Settlement Plan

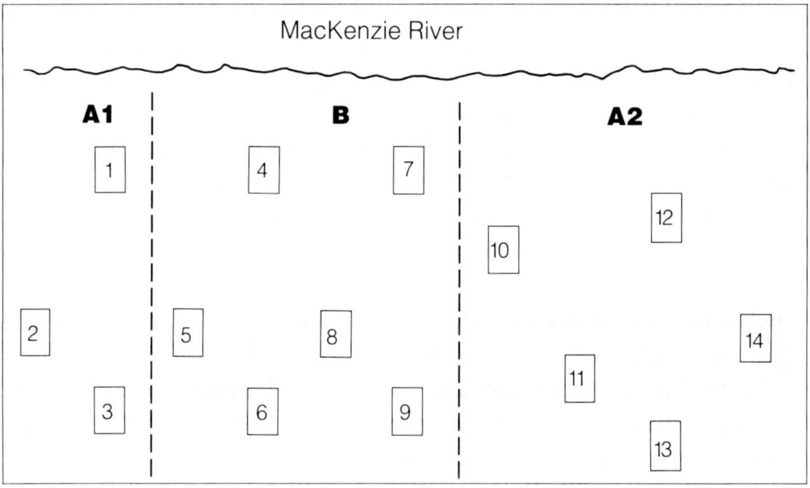

The Kinship Composition Within the Two Primary Pe Tséh Kı́ Groups

An important key to the settlement pattern and to interfamilial relations is found in the kin composition of the two groups. The six women in Group B are related through close biological ties: four are sisters and two are married daughters of the eldest sister. The senior men in Group B are all biologically unrelated but can call each other by the appropriate parallel term to indicate generation. Group B, then, resembles a local band composed of a grouping of sisters married to a grouping of men who call each other brother.

Group A is more complex. Although it contains a group of biological sisters married to a group of biological brothers, Group A also contains opposite sex siblings. These individuals, it would appear, decided to live at the opposite ends of the community from their siblings of the opposite sex; hence, the division of Group A into its two component parts (A1 and A2).

The most complex relationship is that which pertains between Groups A and B. At one level the two groups are tied to each other as affines because the mother of an older woman in Group B was sister to the father of the set of biological sisters in Group A. This description of kinship relations predominated when the Pe Tsʼéh Kį́ people lived for most of the year in autonomous bands, and emphasizes the possibility of intermarriage between the groups.

Since the move into town, attempts have been made to redefine the relationship between groups A and B to one of kinsmen through kinship manipulation (a process that, without unilineal descent to impede reconstruction is endemic to Slavey Dene construction of social space). A partially hypothetical example will illustrate the kind of information that is used to assert the transformation of the relationship between groups A and B. There were two men who called each other brother. One of these men married a woman in Group A. His "brother" established a long-term relationship, equivalent of marriage, with a woman in Group B just after the move into town. This could be interpreted in two ways. In the first interpretation the two groups of women are considered affines and the latter liaison is therefore inappropriate; the men should be affines to one group and kinsmen to the other.[6] The second interpretation assumes that the brothers had married appropriately. Thus the women are considered kinsmen rather than affines, and hence should call each other sister, because they had married brothers. This interpretation, although it alters the kinship patterns of bush living, allows the appearance of a single band composition of the ideal type expressed both verbally and behaviourally in the period prior to the move into Pe Tsʼéh Kį́ – a group of women who call each other sister married to a group of men who call each other brother. However, this view is not firmly established within the community for a variety of reasons: there are continuing tensions between the two groups; many community members disapprove of this liaison; just five years prior to the fieldwork the community had been divided into two kin groups that were clearly *not* related to each other through kin ties. As a result the relationship between the two groups is ambiguous. It seems, simultaneously, either to be composed of one set of kinsmen, and two sets who are not related to each other through parallel ties. This ambiguity creates a dynamic tension between the two groups.

The Social Relations between Households

Social relations between households are governed to a large extent by the nature of the kinship tie between them. The first type of relationship is between those households that are tied through same sex sibling links, and occurs in all groups — B, A1 and A2. The second type is households linked together through opposite sex sibling ties, and occurs in A1 and A2. The third type is between the two large groupings A and B.

Relations between households tied by same sex sibling links are close and behaviour generally follows the pattern described for single households. In particular, the greatest interaction occurs among same sex members while members of the opposite sex are generally avoided. These households are in constant contact and share many activities together. The women frequently go berry picking together, while the men often form hunting parties. Disputes are rare, generally of short duration, and settled with as little publicity as possible.

Relations between Groups A1 and A2 are less clear cut. They share a similar pattern to the first type, in that household members may call each other by parallel terms. In the past seventy years of Pe Tsʼéh Kį band history, however, there have been at least three marriages of persons as closely related through cross kin ties as the present-day members of Groups A1 and A2. This causes ambiguity and can result in visible conflicts. Indeed, contact even between same sex members can be brusque and of short duration, something that does not happen between households linked by parallel ties. Cooperation can turn into conflict, as illustrated by a trapping team consisting of two brothers and their mother's brother's son. Although they worked cooperatively through the fall trapping season, their relationship was reported to be marked by disputes. The team finally broke up during the winter after the cross-cousins almost came to blows.

There are occasions with formal connotations — church services, making the rounds of the households on Christmas or New Year's Day, the New Year's Day feast, the Hand Game and the Drum Dance — during which strong, positive social interaction can take place between Groups A and B. Indeed, as will be outlined in Chapter 7, Drum Dancing can occasionally create a sense of social harmony which reflects the attempted redefinition of the Pe Tsʼéh Kı́ band as an ideal single set of kinsmen. In daily life, however, there is considerable conflict between households in the two groups. Disputes seem chronic; they are publicly articulated and rarely settled, only superceded. Relations between same age, same sex members seem most difficult, though relations between same age, opposite sex members are usually civil and sometimes friendly. This is especially true among the young adults, where relations may lead to romantic involvement. These relationships did not result in intermarriage or long-term relationships. Households of one group are careful to avoid contact with members of the other group in their daily round of activities, and would certainly not voluntarily spend long periods engaged in economic or social tasks together. In short, the structural ambiguity seems to correlate with the dynamic tension between the two groups.

Conclusions

Despite the above discussion, it is possible to describe the Pe Tsʼéh Kı́ band in terms of Helm's (1965) nodal kindred, that is, a grouping organized around cores of closely related individuals of both sexes. From this perspective, the community is composed of two or more primary nodal kindreds (A and B) not closely tied to each other through kinship. Using this model, the location of Groups A1 and A2 in the settlement pattern as well as their relationship are not tied to an underlying structure. In the same way, the avoidance and negative interactions between groups A and B would be seen as the result of previous actions rather than part of a structural pattern. To me, this appropriately describes one dimension of cooperation and conflict within the community: the personal and collective preferences inherent in any social situation.

The second possible way to model Dene bands would conform to a logic of binary opposition associated with the notion of Dravidianate kinship. In this view the world is interpreted on the basis of oppositions between kinsmen and affines or persons whom kinsmen marry. With this orientation the ideal Dene band, at least in the Pe Tséh Kį region, would be composed traditionally of a group of persons who define themselves as kinsmen, and among whom intermarriage would be proscribed. Therefore, the local band would represent one half of a Dravidianate pair and the other half, the affines with whom one intermarried, would reside elsewhere. Needless to say, this other half would not be a numerical fifty percent of the population, for it could greatly outnumber those conceived to be kinsmen. It would be the other half in a conceptual sense only.

This view is supported by the data on band organization, marriage rules described for the period prior to the move into town, and the existence of a Dravidianate terminological system. The closest relations among households exist where there are parallel ties between same sex siblings (hence re-capitulating the ideal), the development of romantic liaisons among members of Groups A and B, and the attempt by members of the community to transform the kinship relationships between the two groups from one in which cross, and therefore marriageable, ties were present to the ideal in which the local band would be composed of kinsmen exclusively.

The perceived band organization of Pe Tséh Kį at the time of this fieldwork contained both views, but was structured ultimately by the second. That is, the community, despite efforts to the contrary, was ultimately conceptualized as containing both halves of the Dravidianate opposition: kinsmen and affines. The existence of such potential marriage partners within local groups did occur in the past, resulting in the transformation of cross-cousins to parallels, thus rendering them unmarriagable. However, the kinship and band organizational system did not anticipate a situation of wholesale, large-scale co-residency among persons related by non-kinsman ties. Consequently, the traditional option of utilizing kinship terminological transformation has not worked well enough to enable the community to conceptualize itself as conforming to the ideal in its interactions in daily life. A traditional binary oppositional orientation under these circumstances would require one of two actions. The first would be to accept intermarriage between members of Groups A and B in spite of the fact that they co-reside. This option has been unsuccessful, largely because of the negative reactions that have taken place in the past. The second option would be to split the community and return to smaller camps. Indeed, some individuals expressed a strong desire to move away from Pe Tséh Kį, although economic factors, such as the lack of small game in the vicinity, were also important influences. Nevertheless, the realities of the situation at the time of this fieldwork made impossible a mass removal either to another community or back to local bands residing in the bush. Hence, the two possible means to overcome the circumstances were blocked.

Under these conditions, one solution would be for the people to define the community in terms of nodal kindreds: that is, the idea that Pe Tsʼéh Kı̨́ is composed of separate communities living side by side. Another response would be to transform the entire kinship system into one that accepts the notion that kinship is tied solely to the immediate biological family and other close biological relatives. This response is reinforced by the importation into the community of Eskimoan terminology as a part of the Euro-Canadian school system. The result may prove to be the demise of any sense of binary opposition within the organization of the next generation of Pe Tsʼéh Kı̨́ residents. Meanwhile, the Drum Dance has become the occasion which affirms that the people living in Pe Tsʼéh Kı̨́ form a single community, by providing an opportunity to overcome the dynamic tensions endemic in the present circumstances.

Footnotes

1. The English translation in quotation marks that immediately follows is an English gloss that is used by the people of Pe Tsʼéh Kı̨́ and is often followed by other equivalents.

2. By "stands in a parallel cousin relationship to ego's father (or mother)" I mean that ego's parent would designate the individual by means of a parallel cousin term.

3. By "stands in a cross-cousin relationship to ego's father (or mother)" I mean that ego's parent would designate the individual by means of a cross-cousin term.

4. Lateral extension also holds for Lynx Point (Helm 1961:70).

5. There is one exception; the women care for all children until they are three or four years old.

6. This liaison could be considered appropriate if the two men are defined as cross-cousins. The possibility that the liaison was inappropriate on kin-based grounds was never raised.

Chapter Four

Kinds of Music and Instruments in Pe Tséh Kį́

Various kinds of music can be heard in Pe Tséh Kį́. Formal music occurs most often in conjunction with specific events such as: The Hand Game, The Church Service, The Curing Ceremony, The Guitar Dance, The Fiddle Dance, and The Drum Dance. Informal music occurs spontaneously, as when an individual who is working alone begins to hum or sing, or when someone is singing a lullaby to an infant. Also, certain event-specific music, such as the Guitar and Fiddle Dance Songs, may be performed informally either by individuals or groups. However, this music is never performed for an audience.

Although almost every adult participates in the production of music, lead performers are generally adult males. There is a clear-cut age differentiation concerning the dance with which an adult male will be associated. For example, leaders for the Guitar Dances are usually 18 to 30 years of age, for the Fiddle Dance usually 30 to 50, and for the Drum Dance generally older than 50.

Instruments

The only instrument used in traditional Dene music is the frame drum (*egheli*). It is constructed as follows: the face of the drum is made from caribou hide stretched around a birch frame with a diameter of roughly two feet. The birch is held together with glue. The caribou is sewn on the frame with sinew strands (*babiche*). Across the outside face of the drum are three strands of *babiche* which make a buzzing sound as the instrument is struck. The instrument is held by means of two strands of *babiche* stretched at right angles across the back of the drum. Attached to the cross made by these strands at the centre of the instrument is a two-inch square also made of pieces of *babiche*. The instrument must be tuned often during a performance. This is done by expanding the caribou skin face over the heat of a fire and then allowing it to cool and contract. The frame drum is struck with a foot long drum stick (*egheli dechį*), made from stripped birch and often larger in circumference at its head. There were four frame drums at Pe Tséh Kį́. They were used in conjunction with drum dancing, hand (or stick) games, and curing ceremonies.

Several other instruments are used by the Pe Tséh Kį́ people. There are approximately four acoustic guitars which are used in conjunction with the Fiddle Dance. There are two violins which are also used in Fiddle Dancing. There are three electric guitars which are used, in combination with voice, at Guitar Dances (social dances in the Euro-Canadian sense). There are also two portable organs; the electric organ belongs to the Roman Catholic church, and the other belongs to the Pentecostal Mission. Neither was used during the period of the fieldwork. Finally, there is an accordian which was never played by its owner.

Musical Occasions

There are seven different types of musical occasions in the community which are briefly described below.

The Hand Game (or Stick Game)

The music for the Hand Game consists of drumming and chanting in monotone and a few unaccompanied songs. Each type of music serves as a background to the action of the game, beginning with the hiding of the token and ending after the guess is made. For the most part, the origin of these songs is unknown.[1] The music of the Easter Hand Game event was recorded; it was the only Hand Game held during the period of the fieldwork.

The Church Service

The music for the church service consists of Euro-Canadian hymns, led by the Priest or Minister, which are sung without accompaniment. One Roman Catholic service was recorded.

The Curing Ceremony

The music for the Curing Ceremony apparently consists of singing and drumming on a Drum Dance drum; however, a ceremony was not observed, and consequently the music was not recorded. The origin of these songs is unknown, but some informants said that they are given to the medicine man by his animal guardian.

Guitar Dance

The music of the Guitar Dance consists of contemporary rock and country songs learned from the radio and records. Guitar Dances occur mainly in the summer when the young adults are in town. There were two Guitar Dances on successive summer Saturdays and a brief dance held on New Year's Day. The music was not recorded.

A drum being played at a Hand Game

Fiddle Dance

The music for the Fiddle Dance, which accompanies either jig or square dances, consists of early fiddle tunes and popular country songs from the period of the 1930s and 1940s. It is said that many of these songs and dances were learned from U.S. servicemen who were stationed at Pe Tséh Kį́ during World War II. The only Fiddle Dance occurred at New Year's. This was not recorded but some Fiddle Dance tunes were recorded out of context. An example appears on Folkways Record FE4541 Side III Band 7 (Asch 1973).

Drum Dance

Drum Dance music consists of a number of songs played with Indian drum accompaniment. Authorship of Drum Dance songs is never claimed by any singer. All songs are attributed to deceased males of high prestige, usually medicine men, and are passed on to the contemporary performers.

The music of the Drum Dance was recorded.[2] A detailed description of this music appears below.

Informal Music

Aside from fiddle tunes played out of context, no informal music was recorded. The authorship of lullabies and hummed tunes is unknown.

Footnotes

1. For a full discussion see Helm and Lurie (1966).

2. The sound recordings of the Drum Dance music and most other music were made using a half-track Tandberg Model 11 portable tape recording with an AKG D-19E microphone. The sound recordings were made at 7 1/2 i.p.s. Some verbal recordings were made on a Sony taperecorder (model number unavailable). Verbal recordings were generally made using Scotch 111 tape. All music was recorded on Scotch 138 tape.

Chapter Five

The Social Organization of the Drum Dance

Drum Dance Occasions

Drum Dances, also known as Tea Dances, are musical events common to all Mackenzie Valley Dene. Although there are few published descriptions, it would appear from the existing information and from personal observation that there is little variation either in musical style or social context from one Dene community or even Dene region to another (Helm 1961:19f, Helm and Lurie 1966:7-12, Kurath 1966:13-22, Mason 1946:28f).

The Drum Dance takes place on formal occasions such as holidays (Christmas, New Year's Day, Treaty Day) or on special occasions such as the men's return from a fall hunt in the bush. They are characterized by: 1) Drum Dancing to the accompaniment of drumming on Indian frame drums; 2) Tea Dancing or dancing in a circle without drum accompaniment; 3) a singing style which emphasizes pulsating vocalization; 4) length, which is a minimum of approximately four hours to a maximum of two or three days. They are events at which all community members are expected to be present.

The Drum Dances are called by various names. One used by the Pe Tséh Kį́ Dene, among other names, is *egheli tsé dahgove* or "dancing to drums." During the fieldwork period, four of the six Drum Dances were held in conjunction with holidays – Christmas, New Year's, and two on Easter. The other two were mounted to mark a special occasion; the one on October 4 celebrated a successful fall hunt undertaken by a large number of Dene men, and the one on April 4 marked the arrival of the mail by dog team from Fort Simpson as part of the activities commemorating the centennial of the Northwest

Territories. They consisted of both Drum and Tea Dances of characteristic style, and lasted upwards of five hours with none lasting longer than one night. In general, all community members attended.

Diagram 5.1 Organization of Space at a Drum Dance

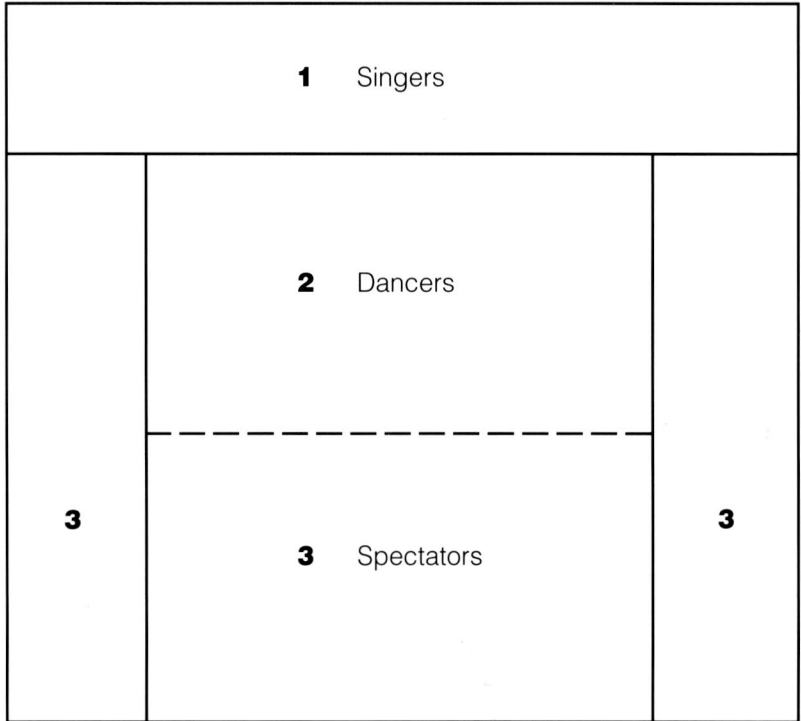

Drum Dances, as the above description indicates, are lengthy, structured events beginning long before the first dance ever takes place. At Pe Tséh Kı́, the process begins about two weeks before with discussions on whether or not there would be a dance and questions of venue. Venue is an important issue, for while Drum Dances can take place outside, in winter it is much more pleasant to have them indoors. However, the only spaces that are large enough to accommodate the community are the community hall and the school, each of which is in the control of a Euro-Canadian administrator. Therefore, the community has to make its request and await a response before knowing for certain where the dance will be. Nonetheless, such a request is never denied and the October 4, Christmas, April 4, and Easter Drum Dances were held in the community hall. The New Year's Day Drum Dance was held at the school because it was accompanied by a feast and required brighter lighting. The first Easter Drum Dance was held in the house of one of the lead singers, for reasons unrelated to the administration of public buildings.

Once a venue is selected, little work is done until the day of the dance. Preparations on that day include cleaning the hall and making a fire outside to tune the frame drum. The time for the dance is set by the singers and generally depends upon the other kinds of festivities taking place in the community. For example, at Christmas there was a party at virtually every house, which meant the dance couldn't begin until late in the evening. Generally, however, the dances begin late in the afternoon or early evening. About an hour before each dance begins, the stove is lit and within half an hour the singers begin to arrive to practice their drumming and singing. From that point on, beginning with the children, the other community members gradually gather. By the time the event gets underway formally, most of the adults planning to attend have arrived.

Regardless of where the dance is held, space is organized in a similar manner. At one end are chairs for the singers who, however, stand when singing. Other participants sit or stand around the perimeter of the other three walls. The centre area is reserved for dancing (see Diagram 5.1).

In Pe Tsʼéh Kį́, all Drum Dances begin with an Opening Song sung in unison by the singers (see song 17), or a speech by one of the singers, or both. The following excerpt from the speech made by one of the lead singers at the start of the second Easter Drum Dance may be considered typical.

> Today is the big day Easter. I am quite pleased that everybody's still healthy and seeing that day again. I hope it will be the same in the future. I am quite happy because we all gathered around today with our children and I hope that they have a good time.
>
> We got no money. We ought to put on a feast for the people but we got no money. The best thing we can do is just have a drum dance or tea dance.
>
> These dance songs are all old songs. We're gonna do some singing with it, those old songs, for the dances. We got no money. But what songs we're going to play with belongs to the old timers and the old days, but what songs they made are still going forward, you know. But we're just going to play some of them we really know best. There might be short-cuts in it, but we'll do our best anyway to play the drum for the dance.

That's all we got left from this land, old timer's songs. But money problem, Indian people, some of them might have money but some of them don't. That's the only problem they have: money.

In the time gone by and in the future coming, I hope all the people have the best of time on big days like Christmas, New Year's and Easter. It doesn't matter about money but as long as we're in good health that's the main part of it.

We're not the boss of our living on this earth here. We don't know when our time is up, but as long as we're in good health we should make the best of everything that comes along, Christmas days and New Year's.

Translation by E.H., July 6, 1970, also H.H. in 1972

The Opening Song has a similar purpose to an opening speech. That is, it is intended to thank God for the singers' good health and to protect the Drum Dance participants from any ill effects that might result from the activities. The singing of this song appears from observation to be directed toward God rather than the participants and, indeed, on the two occasions when it was used, it was performed prior to the arrival of most of the participants.

A Drum Dance at a community hall

Immediately after the speech and/or Opening Song, the dancing begins. There are two major kinds of dances: Drum Dances (*egheli tsé dahgove* or "dancing to drumming") and Tea Dances (*nóláh dahgove* or "sideways dance") – dancing which is not accompanied by drumming. There are two types of Drum Dances: Rabbit Dances (*gah dahgove*) in which a single, even, rhythmical pulse is used (called *nátlale* or "slow beat"; and Cree Dances (*endá dahgove*) in which a duple pulse (called *nátla* or "fast beat") is used.

Diagram 5.2   Drum Dance Diagram

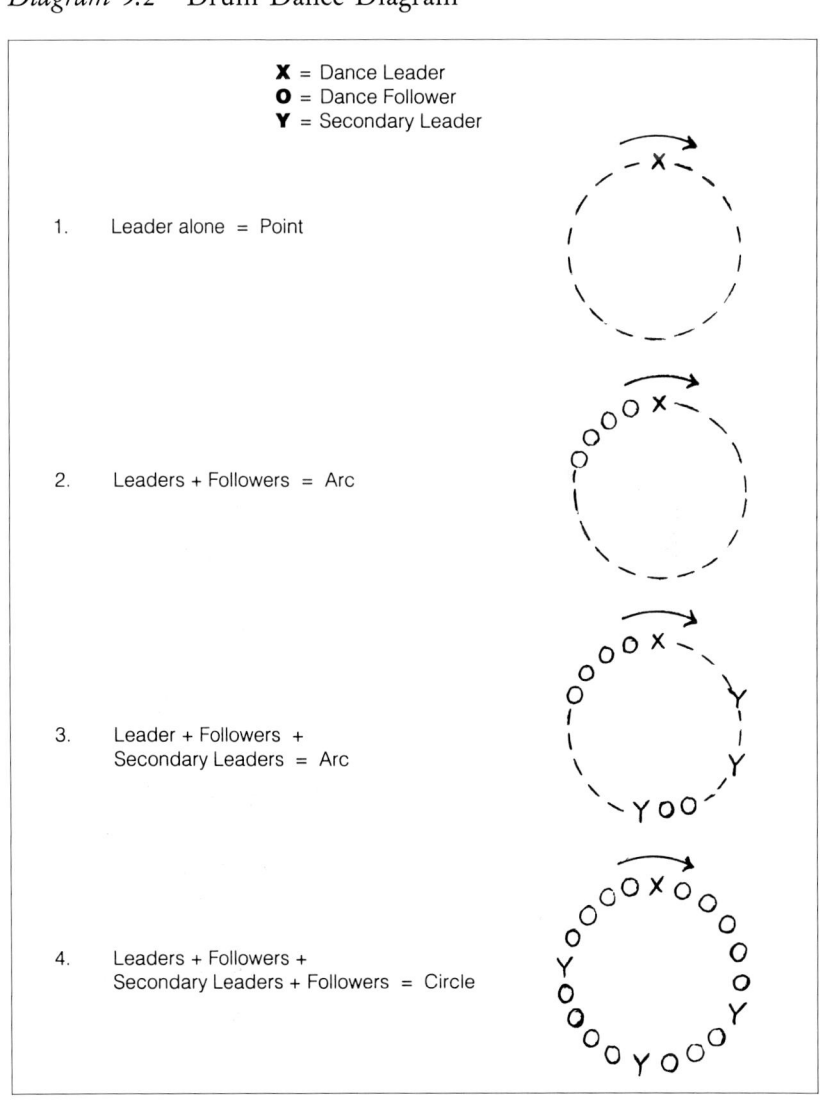

Drum Dance songs — that is, Rabbit and Cree Dance songs as a unit — differ greatly in performance style from Tea Dance songs. Drum Dance songs are characteristically led by a single individual who sings a song in a low voice while drumming lightly. Soon the first dancers begin to move in a clockwise circle in the dance area in front of the singers. At this point, the singers rise, singing and drumming at much higher volume, while other dancers join until there is a circle of people dancing, one behind the other, in the centre of the room. The step follows the beat. The song repeats continually until it is ended, usually by the lead singer, often by using a drum-roll figure and a vocalization which decreases rapidly in pitch. The songs last about four minutes. At this point the singers and dancers return to their seats to await the next song (see Diagram 5.2).

Tea Dance songs, by contrast, are generally group efforts on the part of the singers. They begin with the group of singers seated and singing in low volume while tapping on the frames of their drums. At a certain point, they all rise, put down their drums and move to the dance floor. They begin to circle in a clockwise direction linked arm-to-arm and all facing inwards, forming an arc. Gradually others join them by linking arms and singing. The dance can last at least 10-12 minutes, going through several songs during this period. The performances have no formal endings, but seem to dissipate gradually as people tire of the dance.

According to Helm's account, Drum Dances in Fort Simpson were divided formally into two sections. In the first phase only Drum Dance songs (presumably both Cree and Rabbit) were played. This phase was held indoors, lasting from roughly 9:00 p.m. to perhaps 2:00 or 3:00 a.m. At that point, under proper conditions, the event would be moved outside and Tea Dancing only would take place, lasting until roughly 5:30 to 8:00 a.m.

In Pe Tsʼéh Kį́, during the period of the fieldwork, no Drum Dance shifted venue, nor was there generally any division between the two phases of Drum Dance and Tea Dance. However, as will be discussed in Chapter 7, the people of Pe Tsʼéh Kį́ did perceive such a division in the ideal Drum Dance and did produce two Drum Dances that incorporated it.

In addition to the Opening Song, the two kinds of Drum Dance songs, and the Tea Dance songs, there is a fifth type of musical event during Drum Dances. It consists of an individual humming or singing softly to himself and drumming very lightly on the drum. This occurs throughout the occasion, is ignored by other singers, and is probably not heard by the other participants. There appears to be no Dene word for this type of song, but it is clear from the context that its objective is to enable the singer to practice or warm up his voice; therefore it is referred to here as a Practice Song.

Although Drum Dances can end with formal Closing songs, this did not occur at Pe Tsʼéh Kį́. Rather, events tended to end as people gradually drifted away from the hall and the singers eventually tired of performing.

Performers

Speaking in ideal terms, people respond to questions about who could be singers with the response, "anyone." This, of course, matches their response to questions on the ideal on any subject. However, such a response must be tempered by the fact that both drumming and singing are highly skilled activities which no properly modest person (as a Slavey Dene should be) should undertake without complete preparation. Even acknowledged, skilled singers show proper modesty by apologizing about the possibility of singing well-known songs improperly, as in the case of the lead singer in the opening remarks cited above.

Furthermore, there is no formal mechanism for learning drumming and singing skills, at least at Pe Tsʼéh Kį́. There was, however, one individual who was trying to learn by copying songs he heard the other singers perform. Usually, he did this by following their lead although occasionally he did lead songs himself. Some recordings suggest that his performances on these songs were missing thematic materials.

Given these difficulties, residents of Pe Tsʼéh Kį́ consider themselves lucky to have two men skillful enough to be confident lead singers. Both of these men were raised outside the Pe Tsʼéh Kį́ and later married into it. One is a Dogrib Dene and the other is a Slavey Dene from Fort Norman. Both are in their fifties and live primarily from hunting and trapping in the bush. Although each has at least ten children, one has only one adult son, the other none. As a result, they depend greatly on their own labour to make a living and the Dances are usually held at times when they are recuperating from long stays in the bush. This is one reason why they tend to tire when performing.

Both men learned the songs they sing primarily from Fort Norman people. The Dogrib drummer knows some Dogrib Drum and Tea Dance songs but never performs them at Pe Tséh Kı́ Drum Dances. He learned the songs he performs soon after he arrived in 1946 from a Pe Tséh Kı́ man of great reputation who had learned them himself from Fort Norman people. The Slavey drummer, on the other hand, learned most of his songs from his father.

In addition to these two lead singers, there is one man, a bachelor in his fifties, who lives at Willow Lake River and participates as a lead singer. Unlike the others, he has composed songs (not Drum Dances). Although the origin of his Drum Dance songs is unknown, they appear to be the same as those sung by the other two leaders.

Seven other singers, including the learner, performed at Drum Dances. In general, these performances were restricted to drumming and occasional vocal accompaniment. All of these individuals did on at least one occasion lead a song and all of these singers were men. For the most part, they were over forty and were heads of families. There was one song led by a woman. This took place at a time when a number of people were taking turns in quick succession and was later referred to as "fooling around." It is hard to know if this was done seriously or to prove the point that, ideally, anyone can perform.

In addition to the singers, persons attending Drum Dances can adopt two other fundamental roles. The first of these is the Dancer, of which there are two types. The first is a dance leader, or a person who begins the dancing. Dance leaders possess similar qualities to song leaders in that they are confident in their ability and secure in their place within the community. They differ from drummers in that, at least in Pe Tséh Kı́, they are women. There were two leaders in particular who began most dances; a married woman in her forties, and one in her fifties. The second type of Dancer is the follower, defined as anyone who joins in the dancing. It is, of course, the function of Drum Dances to create dance followers, if not leaders, out of the whole assembly.

The final role is that of Spectator, that is, persons who are present but have not yet become either Dancers or Singers. Of the persons in this category, most are only temporarily in the spectator role with two exceptions; the first is young children and teenagers, especially boys. They function primarily as pranksters whose activities intermittently disrupt the dance. Senior citizens are the second exception. Although they do dance, especially when Tea Dancing takes place or as the occasion wears on, most of the time they sit silently and observe every aspect of the Drum Dance. Their observations form the basis for the official interpretations of the political and social flow of the dance. Often these interpretations differ, resulting in various meanings of the nature of the occasion for the different kin constituencies in Pe Tséh Kį́.

Summary of Types of Musical Activities at Drum Dances

The variation in social behaviours associated with musical activities can be reduced to five identifiable types, easily differentiated by examining changes in activity patterns. To summarize:

Drum Dance (Rabbit Dance): social behaviors.

Singers: Stay in singers' area. A leader leads song. Chorus usually joins in singing after leader begins line.

Dancers: Dancers move into dance area and do a Drum Dance.

Spectators: Little social pressure put on them to participate in dance. Most will stay in spectators' area and either watch the proceedings or gossip. The young men will horse around.

Drum Dance (Cree Dance): social behaviors.

Singers: Stay in singers' area. A leader often sings alone. However, other singers may join in singing.

Dancers: Dancers move into dance area and do a Drum Dance.

Spectators: Same as with Rabbit Dance.

Tea Dance: social behaviors.

Singers: Leave singers' area and become dancers. No lead singer. All sing and dance together as a unit.

Dancers: Dancers move into dance area and do a Tea Dance.

Spectators: Must become dancers. Much social pressure put on them to join in. The young men often find it impossible to avoid dancing a Tea Dance.

Opening Song: social behaviors.

Singers: Stay in singers' area and sing in unison.

Dancers: No dance.

Spectators: Observe or ignore event. Most are just coming into hall.

Practice Song: social behaviors.

Singers: Perform for themselves. Other singers ignore them. Only one drums or sings at a time.

Dancers: No dance.

Spectators: Ignore the event. Usually do not notice it is occurring.

Using the above descriptions, it is possible to develop a table (5.3) to indicate the distinctive social behavioural features for each type of song.

Table 5.3 Social Behaviour/Song Type

| Type | Singers | | Dance Style | Spectator Participation |
	Singing Style	Area Used		
Rabbit	Leader chorus	Singers	Drum Dance	May Dance
Cree	Solo or Leader chorus	Singers	Drum Dance	May Dance
Tea Dance	Unison	Dancing	Tea Dance	Must Dance
Starting	Unison	Singers	No Dance	May Not Dance
Practice	Solo	Singers	No Dance	May Not Dance

This pattern of differentiation in activities will be used in the music analysis to categorize the variety of music sound utterances found in the corpus.

Chapter Six

The Music of the Dene Drum Dance

Very little Dene music has been collected; only Mason's recordings made in 1913 using wax cylinders, and Helm's tapes of Dogrib and Slavey music made in the 1950s and 1960s are on file in the National Museum Archives. In addition, in 1982 Ron Wright collected some Drum Dance and other songs, which are in the archives of the Prince of Wales Museum in Yellowknife.

Until 1975 (Asch 1975a) the only published Dene music descriptions were by Gertrude Kurath (1966). These were based on a corpus of twelve Tea Dance songs and four Drum Dance songs (of the Rabbit Dance type) collected by Helm and Lurie (1966) at a Treaty Day Tea Dance held by the Dogrib Dene at Lac LaMatre in July 1962. She describes the songs as remarkable for their sense of timing and melodic syncopation; using melodic materials highly reminiscent of the tonality of European scales with the colouration of "blues" notes. She also found that the thematic structures had a high degree of organization marked by a simplicity in rhythmic patterns of the beat pulsation. She agrees with Lurie that songs are sung using vocables or non-meaningful sounds, although words may occasionally be added. Finally, she notes frequent instances of pulsation in vocal style. Her only observation on the composition of songs is that the diversity of thematic structuring suggests they may have been composed at different periods and/or by different individuals.

The Drum Dance songs described here are from the Slavey region. They were collected at five of the six Drum Dances which took place at Pe Tséh Kį in 1969-70. Because the drum is often held directly in front of the lead singer's mouth, the recording microphone was placed between the singer and the drum, making the recorded voices of the singers clearer than they were to the audience at the event itself. Some out-of-context recordings were also made of some of the songs. Two singers, and other members of the community, were interviewed on matters such as song composition.

The collection consists of roughly ten hours of material recorded from over one hundred performances of Drum Dance music. Analysis indicates that this corpus represents a total of twenty-two songs, of which eight were Rabbit Dance songs, six were Tea Dance songs, one an Opening Song, and one a Practice Song.

While this appears to be a rather small corpus, one can only speculate on its size relative to the repertoire in other communities. Nevertheless, since it is comparable in size to the Helm and Lurie collection described by Kurath, it probably represents the complete body of material publicly performed in Pe Tséh Kį. Assuming that Lac LaMatre and Pe Tséh Kį are similar in that most songs are performed at each Drum Dance, then the Pe Tséh Kį corpus is about average size for a smaller community with no true specialist in Drum Dance singing.

The small size of the corpus makes it difficult for singers to sequence the Drum Dance songs without repetition. However, by incorporating into each Drum Dance virtually the full repertoire, repetition of songs is reduced to between ten and twenty percent. The sequencing of songs for the New Year's Day Drum Dance illustrates this point (Table 6.1).

Song Composition

Interviews with singers and other individuals elicited the following information on song composition. Although in principle anyone can compose a Drum Dance song, few will take up the challenge and in Pe Tséh Kį no singer said he had composed any Drum Dance song. In fact, the singers often did not know who composed the songs they sang. What is remembered is how and from whom a song was learned.

In discussing the songs in interviews and prior to performances, singers stressed that as a rule songs are "old" in that they come from the "old timers" (the ancestors). Nevertheless, in interviews two composers were mentioned. Victor, a chief at Fort Franklin on Bear Lake, was said to have composed the most frequently performed Tea Dance song (song 18). The composition of eight Drum Dance songs (songs 1, 2, 3, 5, 6, 8, 13, 19) was attributed to Yatsule, born in Fort Norman

Table 6.1 Song Sequence at New Year's Drum Dance

	Performance	Song	Behavioural type
	1	9	Practice
	2	18	Tea Dance
	3	2	Cree
	4	9	Practice
	5	9	Practice
	6	9	Practice
	7	9	Practice
	8	8	Cree
	9	1	Rabbit
	10	5	Cree
	11	9	Practice
	12	N/A	—
	13	1	Rabbit
	14	18	Tea Dance
	15	8	Cree
	16	18	Tea Dance
	17	17	Starting Song
Formal Event Started Here			
	18	3	Rabbit
	19	9	Practice
	20	1	Rabbit
	21	6	Rabbit
	22	2	Cree
	23	1	Rabbit
	24	18	Tea Dance
	25	8	Cree
	26	18	Tea Dance
	27	21	Tea Dance
	28	20	Tea Dance
	29	3	Rabbit
	30	1	Rabbit
	31	18	Tea Dance
	31A	18	Tea Dance
	32	21	Tea Dance
	33	16	Cree
	34	7	Rabbit
	35	3	Rabbit
	36	2	Cree
	37	6	Rabbit
	38	22	Tea Dance
	39	22	Tea Dance
	40	18	Tea Dance
	41	6	Rabbit
	42	18	Tea Dance
	43	2	Cree
	44	1	Rabbit
	45	7	Rabbit

in 1879. Some of those interviewed said that Yatsule composed all of his songs on his death bed, although others considered this doubtful.

Generally speaking, it would appear that songs are not known by title. In interviews they were described by function and, where applicable, by composer. Titles which appear to describe the individual songs were provided by consultants after detailed questioning, but must be viewed as tentative at best. Such titles as were given generally signified the notion of gift to the audience, underscoring the functional nature of the song in giving with the sense of reciprocity that permeates Dene ideology.

Non-singers suggested, in one case most strongly, that as a rule Drum Dance songs (like all Dene songs) must have words. Singers, on the other hand, were more cautious, agreeing that songs should have words, but they were often unknown. This was attributed by one non-singer to the imitative style of learning. He suggested that, given the loudness of the drumming in relation to the singing, it would be hard for the person learning the song to catch the words. He maintained that only the composer would know the words with any certainty.

The following is a list of phrases, provided by an observer at the performances, that appear to be used occasionally in the course of songs.

denecho dahsahteh	=	a big man is holding me up
máhsicho	=	thank you very much
ezhie	=	downwards
di ndéh keh gonezį	=	everything is good in this world

Whether or not these were the words pronounced by the singers themselves, when singing, could not be ascertained even after specific questions were posed.

Another aspect of this question was whether the words occurred in specific places in the song or were simply repeated at random. Interviewees indicated that the latter is more often the case. At Pe Tséh Kį, as at Lac LaMatre, Drum Dance songs are usually performed using vocables. Unfortunately, these sounds could not be accurately described by the singers because they found it hard to reproduce them without singing and drumming at the same time. Although it was difficult for the singers to specify verbal descriptions of the organization of the melodic aspects of the songs, they were able to describe the drum beat, pointing out the opposition of *nátla* (fast) to *nátlale* (slow).

The Organization of Music Sound

This interpretation of Pe Tsʼéh Kı̨́ Drum Dance music relies on the existence of a correspondence between certain Dene ideas about music sound, as exemplified in performance and general descriptions, and western ones. This correspondence, which may appear to be obvious and commonsensical, may not in fact be unambiguously true universally. The fundamental proposition is that the basic unit of Dene music sound, like the "song" in western music, contains a unique bundle of music sounds which is repeated within a performance and can be clearly separated from non-music sound. The following points of correspondence can be derived from this fundamental proposition:[1]
1. Like Western music, Dene music contains the notion of a melodic scale.
2. Like Western music, Dene music contains the notion of a melody.
3. Like Western music, Dene music contains the notion of metric rhythm.

Drum Dance Song Structure

Slavey Scale

An examination of the songs indicates that the Slavey scale can be conceptualized as containing six fundamental tones. These tones are very similar to the European major scale, but with the seventh tone omitted and the third and sixth tones are flattened, as compared to the major tempered scale. This flattening corresponds to the tonal placement that Kurath described as "blues notes." Of the twenty-one songs in the corpus, one used the range of a major third, thirteen a fifth, two a major sixth, and five an octave.

Melody

Melodies are structurally based on a relationship between a sequence of higher tones and a foundation or ground tone, the latter parallel to the tonic in the Euro-Canadian scale. Melodies generally follow a descending pattern, beginning at or very near the highest tone in the song and moving downwards toward the foundation tone, where they remain for long periods before swooping up again. Only one melody descended below the foundation tone.

All songs can be divided into two formal parts. The Theme Section (labelled T) is a section of tonal variation; the Rest Section (labelled R) is the the section in which the melody remains at rest on the tonic (foundation or ground tone). The pattern of the melody in the Rest Sections appears to be similar to the pulsations on the tonic which Kurath described in the Dogrib material. In Pe Tsếh Kị́ the sounds in this section of the melody are not so much pulsated as they are sung in a manner similar to contemporary Euro-Canadian music.

Melodies are composed of up to three short Theme Sections. A Theme Section often contains smaller units or phrases and might be made up of one or two of these units (labelled a, b). In melodies with more than one Theme Section, the final phrase of each Theme Section was identical (labelled f). Rest Sections are of two types: those in which the tonal sequence was repeated identically throughout the performance (labelled y), and those in which it varied as the length within it (labelled x). The former type was usually sung in the vocable *he*; the latter with the vocable *ha*.

All songs conform at the highest level of abstraction to an alternating theme-rest section pattern (or ||:TR:||). At the most precise level of melodic organization, eight unique types can be identified (Diagram 6.2). It should be noted that many Drum Dance song performances had an ending formula. This consisted of a vocal glissando matched with a drum roll, often ending with a spoken *máhsi* or "thank you."

Diagram 6.2   Melodic Structures

1. ||:afxbfx:|| (6 songs)
2. ||:afxfx:|| (6 songs)
3. ||:ay:|| (3 songs)
4. ||:afxbfxafx:|| (1 song)
5. ||:ax:|| (1 song)
6. ||:afy:|| (1 song)
7. ||:afxfxbfx:|| (1 song)
8. ||:afybfy:|| (1 song)

For two songs, the recordings were too poor to ascertain the melodic structure.

Beat Pulsation

Three kinds of beat patterning were found in the corpus. The first consisted of even beat pulsations of even stress that occurred roughly at quarter note intervals. The second consisted of a duple figure that sounded almost like a grace note followed by a beat of roughly quarter note duration. The final beat pattern consisted of even beat pulsations occurring at quarter note intervals, with an uneven stress pattern. The three types can be described in Diagram 6.3 below.

Diagram 6.3   Rhythmic Structures

Type A   ‖: ♩̌♩̌ :‖
Type B   ‖: ♩̃♩ :‖
Type T   ‖: ♩̌♩ :‖

Description of the Music Sounds

Each of the following twenty-two descriptions contains an indication of tonal range, melodic structure, beat pattern, and the type of social setting. Other relevant information derived from discussions

with the members of the community is also included. The melodic sketches, which have all been transposed to a foundation tone of G below middle C, are reproduced in Appendix B. A complete description of a performance of one song appears in Appendix A.

Song 1

    Tonal Range: 5th
    Melodic Structure: afxfx
    Beat Pattern A
    Song Type: Rabbit Dance

    According to one non-singer, this song may be called *séot'į nee k'eh* (on my people's land). In one performance the same individual thought the singers might be saying *denecho dahsahteh* (A big man is holding me up). In another version, he thought words might include *máhsicho nehfe* (I want to thank you very much). This song, which was performed at each Drum Dance recorded, was attributed by one of the singers to Yatsule. It was performed a total of eleven times. A recording of one performance of this song appears on Side 3, Band 5 of Folkways Record FE4541 (Asch 1973).

Song 2

    Tonal Range: 5th
    Melodic Structure: afxfx
    Beat Pattern B
    Song Type: Cree Dance

    According to one singer this song may be known as the *nátegozhį* (prophet's song) or *dahgove mezhį* (dance song). A non-singer identified this as *séot'į nee k'eh* (on my people's land). One individual thought they were saying *ezhie* (downwards) in one performance and *séot'į máhsicho* (thank you my friends) in another. The one singer interviewed said the song had no words. This song, which is also attributed to Yatsule, appears to be popular since it was sung at each dance and was performed a total of twelve times. A singer commented that when he performed this song in Fort Norman the drumming seemed to be too fast for the dancers.

    A recording of one performance of this song appears on Side 2, Band 6 of Folkways Record FE4541 (Asch 1973). In this performance, the third tone of the Slavey scale was less pronounced than in other performances. As well, the Rest Section between the themes is regular enough that it might be diagramed as afyfx.

Song 3
Tonal Range: 5th
Melodic Structure: afxbfx
Beat Pattern A
Song Type: Rabbit Dance

According to one non-singer, words might include *di ndéh ke'h gok'eh* (on this land) or *di ndéh ke'h gonezį* (everything is good on this land). This song, too, is attributed to Yatsule. It was performed eight times and was considered by the non-singer to be the most popular Drum Dance song.

Song 4
There is no precise transcription of this song because the one performance was very short and so hard to follow that the melodic structure could not be determined. However, it used an A-type beat pattern. According to one individual this song may be a gambling song that was mixed in.

Song 5
Tonal Range: 5th
Melodic Structure: afxbfx
Beat Pattern B
Song Type: Cree Dance

This song was identified as perhaps having the title *séot'į máhsicho* (thank you my friends). However, according to the non-singer interviewed it has no words. Two singers attributed this song to Yatsule. It was performed six times.

Song 6
Tonal Range: 5th
Melodic Structure: afxbfxafx
Beat Pattern A
Song Type: Rabbit Dance

The non-singer interviewed thought the title might be "oh my friends, let's go dancing." He said there were some words to it but he could not make them out. The song was attributed to Yatsule and was performed seven times.

Song 7
Tonal Range: octave
Melodic Structure: afxbfx

Beat Pattern A
Song Type: Rabbit Dance
The title is not known. Some people said it had words but no one knows them. The song was performed four times.

Song 8
Tonal Range: octave
Melodic Structure: afxfx
Beat Pattern B
Song Type: Cree Dance
The non-singer interviewed said the song has words, but he could not make them out. A singer interviewed agreed that there were words, but he did not know them. The song is attributed to Yatsule and was performed eight times.

Song 9
Tonal Range: 6th
Melodic Structure: ax
Beat Pattern A
Song Type: Practice
One person said that the song might be very old, or it might be Euro-Canadian, "because on the radio you hear some songs from the white man's side." In any case, he had never heard it before. Similarities to Navajo material — played for the people of Pe Tséh Kį during the period of fieldwork — were observed. The song was performed seven times, mostly at the New Year's Day Drum Dance. On one occasion, an individual learning to be a singer used it as a dance song, but the dance stopped amid loud laughter, especially from the other singers. It was performed once by a woman who used a B-type beat pattern.

Song 10
Tonal Range: 5th
Melodic Structure: afxbfx
Beat Pattern A
Song Type: Rabbit Dance
The non-singer interviewed thought there might be words to it. It was performed once.

Song 11
    Tonal Range: 5th
    Melodic Structure: afxbfx
    Beat Pattern A
    Song Type: Rabbit Dance
    The non-singer interviewed said that there were words but he did not follow them. One singer said he learned the song in Yellowknife or Fort Rae and has heard it performed in Fort Norman. This song was performed three times.

Song 12
    There was no precise melodic transcription due to the poor quality of the performance. However, the tonal range is a fifth and the beat pattern is A-type. It was used in Rabbit Dancing. The non-singer interviewed believed the title might be *yakegotine* (far away or far away people). He said it had no words.

Song 13
    Tonal Range: Octave
    Melodic Structure: afxfx
    Beat Pattern B
    Song Type: Cree Dance
    The non-singer thought the song had no words, but was in the style of the prophet's song (see Song 2). The song was attributed to Yatsule and was performed five times.

Song 14
    Tonal Range: 5th
    Melodic Structure: afy
    Beat Pattern T
    Song Type: Tea Dance
    The non-singer said that this song had no words. It was performed once.

Song 15
    Tonal Range: 5th (but goes to D below G in Rest Section)
    Melodic Structure: ay
    Beat Pattern T
    Song Type: Tea Dance

Song 16
    Tonal Range: 5th
    Melodic Structure: afxfx
    Beat Pattern B
    Song Type: Cree Dance
    The song was performed twice.

Song 17
    Tonal Range: major 6th
    Melodic Structure: afxfxbfx
    Beat Pattern A
    Song Type: Opening Song
    According to the non-singer interviewed, this song is used only for the starting of a Drum Dance. It is somewhat like a prayer for help in drumming; therefore it is not danced to. It comes from Fort Norman.

Song 18
    Tonal Range: 5th
    Melodic Structure: afxbfx
    Beat Pattern T
    Song Type: Tea Dance
    According to a non-singer, the title of the song might be "everybody dance now" or "hello my friends everybody is dancing." According to one of the singers, Victor, a chief at Fort Franklin, made up the song on a trip to Fort Rae and Yellowknife, saying at the time, "There is nothing to be shy about when you see different people. The only thing to do is not to be shy but to entertain strangers." The song, according to one singer, can be used for Drum or Tea Dancing. It was the most popular Tea Dance song and was performed fifteen times.

Song 19
    Tonal Range: octave
    Melodic Structure: afxfx
    Beat Pattern B
    Song Type: Cree Dance
    This song is attributed to Yatsule. It was performed twice. In one performance led by the learner, who forgot the proper structure, it was sung afxafx.

Song 20
    Tonal Range: 5th
    Melodic Structure: ay
    Beat Pattern T
    Song Type: Tea Dance
    The song was performed once, but since the recording was poor, the transcription may not be precise.

Song 21
    Tonal Range: major 3rd
    Melodic Structure: ay
    Beat Pattern T
    Song Type: Tea Dance
    The song was performed twice.

Song 22
    Tonal Range: 5th
    Melodic Structure: afybfy
    Beat Pattern T
    Song Type: Tea Dance
    The song was performed twice. The recording is of poor quality.

Relation between Form and Function in Drum Dance Songs

    The five kinds of social activities associated with the production of music sounds at a Drum Dance are: Rabbit Dances, Cree Dances, Tea Dances, Opening Songs, and Practice Songs. The following analysis describes the correlation between various features of music sound in the twenty-two songs and the five kinds of events at which they are utilized. The intention is to determine whether there are markers in the music that indicate the specific function for which a song is intended. This hypothesis is proposed because the interviewees tended to label songs by their function, and because each song is typically associated with only one type of activity; for example, a song described as a Rabbit Dance song was used only for Rabbit Dancing.

Chart 6.4   Types of Song/Number of Different Songs

Rabbit Dance	4
Cree Dance	6
Tea Dance	6
Starting Song	1
Practice song	1
Unknown	1
Total	22

Chart 6.5   Tonal Range/Song Type

	Rabbit	Cree	Tea	Starting	Practice
3rd			1		
5th	6	3	4		
6th				1	1
8th	1	3	1		

Chart 6.6   Rhythmic Pattern/Song Type

	Rabbit	Cree	Tea	Starting	Practice
Type A	7			1	1
Type B		6			
Type C			6		

Chart 6.7   Melodic Phrase Structure/Song Type

	Rabbit	Cree	Tea	Starting	Practice
1. afxbfx	5	1	1		
2. afxfx	1	5			
3. ay			3		
4. afxbfxafx	1				
5. ax					1
6. ay			1		
7. afxfxbfx				1	
8. afybfy			1		

As Charts 6.5, 6.6, and 6.7 indicate, there was a high degree of consistency in the features of tonal range, melodic phrase structure, and rhythmic accompaniment among songs in a particular category. Specifically, Rabbit Dance Songs typically utilized a tonal range of a fifth, a melodic structure with two thematic sections of equal phrase length divided by x-type Rest Sections, and a duple beat pattern with even stress accents. Rabbit Dance Songs also typically ended in a sequence beginning with a drum roll, continuing with a rapid vocal glissando over the drum roll, and concluding with a strongly stated *máhsi* or *máhsicho* (thank you or thank you very much) at the end of the glissando.

Cree Dance Songs had a melodic range that varied between a fifth and an octave, with a characteristic melodic structure of two themes of uneven phrase length, the second theme being a repeat of the final phrase in the first theme. The beat stress pattern used the triplet figure with a longer stress beat and a shorter unaccented one. As in the Rabbit Dance Songs, the themes were divided by x-type Rest Sections and ended in characteristic sequences.

There was a much higher degree of variation in the Tea Dance Songs than in any other type, although there was still one predominant pattern. Typically, Tea Dance songs used the tonal range of a fifth, a melodic structure that consisted of a single, one-phrase theme separated by beat sections of even duration, and a rhythmic pattern of duple beats with uneven stress.

The Practice Song used the tonal ranges of a sixth, a melodic structure that consisted of one phrase theme separated by Rest Sections of uneven length, and a duple beat pattern with even stress. In contrast, the Starting Song, which also used a tonal range of a sixth and a duple beat pattern with even stress, consisted of a melodic structure that consisted of three thematic sections of varying length separated by uneven Rest Sections.

Footnotes

1. This approach follows the orientation toward analysis found in structural linguistics (Lyons 1969). Fundamentally there are three components, the first of which may be called "performance" or "phonetics." Here, the music is examined as though each musical utterance (i.e., performance) is a unique, unrepeated event. In this way it is possible to establish the total number of performances, the range of pitches used in them, and the fundamental melodic and rhythmic structure found in the corpus. The second component may be called "song" or "phonemics" and analyzes the elements of melodic and rhythmic organization. The third component, "song types" or "morphology and syntax" examines the relationship between the structural organization of the songs and the specific social context or event in which they occurred; that is, the relationship between formal structure and, for example, the type of dance for which it is used.

Chapter Seven

On the Meaning of the Drum Dance

Having examined the relationship between the social context of song production and the formal musical properties of each song in the Drum Dance, this chapter explores the meaning of the occasion itself in terms of the social solidarity that arose when a Drum Dance was successfully performed. This solidarity helped to create the sense that, despite their origins in different local bands, the Slavey Dene of Pe Tséh Kĺ still constitute a community. In this way a successful Drum Dance reinforced the idea that Pe Tséh Kĺ could be conceptualized as a single local band created through the kinship transformations discussed in Chapter 3. It is suggested that a successful Drum Dance is not preordained, but depends upon the cooperative efforts of the participants in the production of the Drum Dance.

In this chapter, the following questions are answered.
1. What is the ideal of a successful Drum Dance?
2. What are the conditions necessary for its creation?
3. What is the process through which the ideal Drum Dance is achieved?
4. What are the ways in which the meaning of a successful Drum Dance is communicated to the participants?

The Ideal Drum Dance as a Musical Occasion

Marcia Herndon (1971:340) has defined a musical occasion as "an encapsulated expression of the shared cognitive forms and values of a society.... It is usually a named event, with a beginning and an end, varying degrees of organization of activity, audience/performance and location." The purpose of the Drum Dance is to celebrate the arrival of important persons to the community, to commemorate important calendrical events, and to acknowledge the return of kinsmen. While this remains true in an external sociological sense, at a more symbolic level the Drum Dance has as its purpose something much more profound. Savishinsky, in a discussion of the Drum Dance among the Hare Indians (a neighbouring Athapaskan-speaking group), suggested that "Drum Dancing at the village [of Coleville Lake] is a cathartic display of ritualized energies, drawing together the efforts and sentiments of the entire band, and epitomizing the collective force of each reunion" (1974:130). This "desired purpose" of the Drum Dance can only be achieved by the proper performance of the musical occasion, and comes much closer to the sense of shared cognitive forms and values suggested in Herndon's definition.

As described earlier, Drum Dances begin with a speech and/or an Opening Song followed by dances of three kinds: Rabbit Dances (*gah dahgove*) in which the singer-drummers remain in a single area and the dancers move to a duple meter in a circular fashion, one behind the other but never touching; the Cree Dance (*endá dahgove*) which is similar except the dance is based on a triple meter; and Tea Dances (*nóláh dahgove*) in which the singer-drummers start the song, then lay down their drums to dance, holding hands and facing the centre, thus forming an arc; the other participants join in to complete the circle. The typical Drum Dances end when people tire or become bored with the occasion.

The Qualities of the Ideal Drum Dance

Although the ideal Drum Dance begins and ends in the same manner as the typical dance (see also Helm, 1961), in between there are two dancing sections rather than one. These are: the Drum Dance proper (*egheli dahgove*) in which predominantly Rabbit Dances and Cree Dances are performed; and, after a long period of time, the Tea Dance proper (*nóláh dahgove*) in which only Tea Dances are performed.

Of the six Drum Dance musical occasions which took place during this field work, only the October 4 Drum Dance and the April Drum Dance achieved the ideal. The four unsuccessful Drum Dances were the Christmas Day Drum Dance, the one held at New Year's, and both the afternoon and evening Drum Dances held on Easter Day.

The ideal Drum Dance requires desire, competence, and a willingness to lay aside personal disputes in order to create a special world out of the roles and behaviours available within the Drum Dance social context. The first quality was a strong commitment on the part of the participants and especially the singer-drummers. In the case of the second Easter Drum Dance this was the only condition not met because some of the people (particularly one lead singer) were too tired after a night of Hand-Gaming and an earlier abortive attempt to start a Drum Dance. The Dance began well enough, but stopped abruptly in the middle when one lead singer left the hall.

The second quality is competence: the performers and especially the song leaders must be skilled at playing and singing. The Christmas Drum Dance failed, despite a strong sense of motivation, because in the absence of one of the two major song leaders a beginner incorrectly sang all the songs he led, by singing only parts of the songs in a repetitious manner.

Although the third quality is more difficult to explain, it is the most important of the three. It may be described as the willingness of the participants to create a special world out of the roles and social behaviours of the Drum Dance musical occasion, a world in which the conflicts contained in daily social life are suspended for a moment and a communal "we rationale" (Goffman 1961:18) prevails. This quality is the most difficult to achieve, because this world must be built by the very same people with whom disputes occur in daily life. In the case of the New Year's Drum Dance this was made impossible by the introduction of the contentious issue of the election of a Chief by one of the song leaders who happened to be a candidate. The afternoon Easter Drum Dance was held at the house of the same song leader, and it was obvious from the low attendance that most people felt the political dispute was too hot to be kept out of a Drum Dance at his house, despite attempts to ignore it.

The Achievement of the Ideal Drum Dance

The question of the process by which an ideal Drum Dance is achieved can be divided into two parts: the creation of this special world and the conditions under which it is most likely to occur.

In the typical Drum Dance, Drum and Tea Dance songs are performed in no particular order; in the ideal Drum Dance there are two distinct sections, a long Drum Dance section followed by a long Tea Dance section. The Drum Dance phase lays the groundwork for the Tea Dance phase. In the Drum Dance phase, the singer-drummers perform songs in an effort to get spectators to dance. Participation is still voluntary; by dancing participants signal approval of the direction of the musical occasion. If they approve by dancing to most Drum Dance songs, eventually the song leaders will begin the Tea Dance phase characterized by continuous dancing with no obvious leadership and participation by the entire community.

Looking at this process from a more structural point of view, the people in the Drum Dance phase belong to two opposed groups: singers, who are engaged in the event, and other participants, who are more often spectators. The objective, then, of this phase is to transform the spectators into engaged participants by getting them to dance. An analysis of the Drum Dances indicates that this can only be accomplished when the singers show, through their speechmaking and their sharing of song leadership, that they have already achieved the integrative we rationale. After a while, the others signal their approval and willingness to enter this special world by dancing, the spectators becoming engaged performers. When all the spectators are engaged performers the Tea Dance has begun. In this phase the opposition between the roles of singer-drummer and dancer are overcome as the singer-drummers transform themselves into dancers.

On some occasions, however, the singer-drummers do not meet these expectations, or the external political matters within the community are too distracting. Under these conditions people tend not to dance to the Drum Dance songs, forcing the singer-drummers to introduce Tea Dance songs prematurely. This is done in an effort to attain at least the manifest function of the Drum Dance which is to dance. On a latent level, this signals to all the impossibility of attaining the special world status through the process of the ideal Drum Dance.

In the successful Drum Dance of 4 October 1969, eighteen of twenty-two consecutive Drum Dance songs were danced to before the first Tea Dance song was performed; this took approximately two hours. At the unsuccessful New Year's Drum Dance, the first Tea Dance song took place after the performance of only five Drum Dance songs, none of which were danced to; only half an hour had passed. The same pattern holds true for all unsuccessful Drum Dances except for the Evening Easter one which failed, even though eight consecutive Drum Dance songs were performed and danced to, because the lead singer was tired. In all cases the same song was used as the first Tea Dance song, presumably because it theoretically could be used for either a Rabbit Dance or a Tea Dance, allowing the drummers to mask their defeat with one more effort that could be ambiguous and hence danced, if they are lucky, as a Drum Dance.

Comparing the two successful Drum Dances with the four unsuccessful ones, two conditions become apparent. First, both successful Drum Dances took place for the benefit of outsiders. The April Drum Dance was held to honour the people bringing mail by dog team from Fort Simpson to Pe Tsʼéh Kį́ as part of the celebrations marking the centennial year. The decision to hold the October Drum Dance, which nominally took place because the hunters had returned from a fall hunt, was also influenced by the recent arrival of this researcher into the community. In contrast, all four unsuccessful Drum Dances were held to commemorate the return to Pe Tsʼéh Kį́ of members of the community. Second, successful Drum Dances apparently occurred at unpredictable times, whereas unsuccessful ones occurred on calendrically predicted days. Thus an element of surprise may also be a desirable condition, but not a necessary one, as in other years the New Year's, Christmas, Easter, and Treaty Day Drum Dances may have been successful.

The Creation of a We Rationale

The desired purpose of the ideal Drum Dance is to epitomize the collective unity of the community (Savishinsky 1974). Through the resources available in the Drum Dance, the conflicts inherent in daily life are replaced for a moment by a special world characterized by an integrative we rationale. This can be achieved only if there is proper motivation, skill, and most importantly, a willingness on the part of the participants to suspend their conflicts. The suspension of conflicts is easiest when the Dance is held to honour outsiders and when there is little warning. This special world is achieved through a process which moves the participants from the Opening Song phase, in which singers are the only ones engaged; through the Drum Dance phase, in which the other participants progressively become engaged by dancing; to the Tea Dance phase, in which leadership is overwhelmed as universal participation is achieved.

Savishinsky suggests that communication of this we rationale is contained in the Dance itself, since "Drum Dances are exuberant and hypnotic in their communal and rhythmic movement" (1974:127). In part this is true and is reflected in the very structure of the dance songs in particular. However, it is incomplete since not all Drum Dances produced this result. A central component that must be present is the process of social exchange within the event itself. In the Drum Dance phase the process involves social exchanges among the singer-drummers regarding song leadership, and also between singer-drummers and others concerning dancing; in the Tea Dance phase, the process involves the role transformation of singers into dancers. For the event to progress, the outcome of these exchanges must emphasize cooperation — a fundamental quality perceived as necessary to create a sense of community. In the first exchange, cooperation is tested by the possibility of competition over leadership among the singer-drummers and is asserted when there is sharing of leadership in starting and performing Drum Dance songs. In the second exchange, cooperation is tested by the possibility that non-singers may exercise their right not to participate and is asserted when they dance to Drum Dance songs. In the Tea Dance phase, cooperation is affirmed when the singer-drummers leave their private space and move onto the dance floor to create a single circle of dancers. Thus, it is in these exchanges, as well as the dancing and the music, that the communication of the we rationale is created.

Conclusions

To the participants, the social implications of achieving an ideal Drum Dance involve ritual, not in the sense of a religious ceremony, but rather, as Murphy says (1971:243), to "bridge the contradiction between norm and action and mediate the alienation of man from his fellow man."

As the evidence indicates, the bridge Murphy describes is neither preordained nor predefined by the very fact that a Drum Dance occurs, but is contingent upon the actions of the people who assemble and proceed through the occasion together. Since this bridge is constructed with the very persons with whom discord may occur in daily life, the actions of individuals can at any point prevent the attainment of the special world of the ideal Drum Dance. For the people of Pe Tšéh Kį́ the step-by-step and dance-by-dance achievement of the ritual provides a profound confirmation of potential community strength and resilience.

Postscript

A Perspective from 1988

When living in Pe Tsʼéh Kį́, I was strongly aware of the sense of community arising from the Drum Dance as described in Chapter 7. My dissertation, however, an analytical treatise on methodology focussing on the structure and organization of music sound, was not as successful as I would have liked: the analysis of music sound that was appropriate to the Slavey Dene remained to a large degree out of my grasp. In part, the reason for this was contained in the elusive nature of music sound itself. Music differs greatly from language in that a rendering appropriate to the way in which people hear the sounds still is not possible for most musics, making any attempt at description arbitrary.

The first draft of Chapter 7 (1975), finally described the strong, positive emotive flow of the event in Pe Tsʼéh Kį́ that had escaped my earlier work. However, although it accurately reflected one component of Pe Tsʼéh Kį́ social life — the urge to create community — it read as though the Drum Dance, when successful, embodied a necessary (and perhaps sufficient) verification of that desire. This interpretation of the Drum Dance was one-sided. It ignored the fact that the creation of a community in the immediate present might undermine the possibility for social reproduction. After all, if the meaning of the Drum Dance was to create a single local band out of what once was a regional band, it was decreasing greatly the possibility for intermarriage among community members. In other words, it ignored the possibility that a "successful" Drum Dance could connote a negative long-term consequence whereas an "unsuccessful" Drum Dance, which in a sense denied "community," could connote a positive long-term result.

To discover whether such a hypothetical concern was real to the people of Pe Tsʼéh Kį́ was, like the appropriate analysis of music sound, something I felt was beyond my grasp. All I can say with certainty is that at the moments when the dances took place in 1969 and 1970, the sense of community I interpreted seemed to be felt as strongly by the people of Pe Tséh Kį́ as it was by me.

There was a second shortcoming of my analysis of the meaning of the Drum Dance. In 1969, I saw the community as attempting to resolve its difficulties and to create a social life in highly changed circumstances through internal means alone. Yet although the Pe Tséh Kį́ people were using their own resources (such as the ability to manipulate kin terms and the use of the Drum Dance) to create and recreate their social universe in new circumstances, these efforts seemed only of immediate efficacy, bound for failure in the long-term. In other words, my analysis gave me a negative impression that belied the feelings I experienced in the Drum Dance.

This apparent contradiction has been resolved by more recent events. In Pe Tséh Kį́ in 1969-70 little attention was directed toward resolving external causes of problems faced by the community, such as government policy, although people would discuss government betrayal of solemn treaty agreements. They were also well aware that the government had reneged on more recent commitments of free rent, water, and wood, promised as incentives for the move to Pe Tséh Kį́. Some young men, angered by the way they had been treated at high school in Yellowknife, expressed an analogy between the circumstances of the Dene and those of the Vietnamese people. Perhaps because government seemed so distant and so powerful, the focus of adaptation in 1969 was primarily on community resources. The people of Pe Tséh Kį́ seemed to accept the imposed conditions as determinants with which they had to cope.

By the mid 1970s, the Dene Nation, and the Pe Tséh Kį́ people in particular, had changed. They were aware that the solution of the negative aspects of their current economic, social, and political situation required fundamental change in their relationship with the Canadian state and its development policy. By this time the anger of the few and the rarely expressed unease of the many had been transformed into actions, such as a blockade to stop mineral developers from moving into the Pe Tséh Kį́ area and a decision to oppose the continuation of the all-weather highway from Fort Simpson to Pe Tséh Kį́. This has been followed by a continuing opposition to the Mackenzie Valley Pipeline, and by the demand for self-government.

This process, of course, was not unique to Pe Tséh Kį́. In the early 1970s the Dene, through the Indian Brotherhood of the Northwest Territories (now called the Dene Nation), successfully forced the Canadian government to re-open treaty negotiations by proving that the written versions of the treaties were inaccurate. The Dene Declaration of 1975 (Asch 1985:127f) asserts their national political rights and need to negotiate a political relationship with Canada. Similarly, at the Berger hearings, they voiced formal objections to massive development on their land prior to the settlement of their outstanding claims. Clearly, the Dene communities were at last confronting the primary external agents of change: the Canadian state and the corporate developers.

Thus these recent developments bring a new perspective to the analysis of Pe Tśéh Kį́ social organization in 1969. The Drum Dance, as it was successfully performed at that time, the creation of the mature household as the form of economic adaptation, and the manipulation of kinship to assert local band organization for the community as a whole, all demonstrate an important matter — a community can exclusively use its own cultural forms as a means to fend off the negative impacts of imposed change only for a time. At least in the case of Pe Tśéh Kį́, such acts are inherently temporary, for they create resolutions in the immediate present at the cost of the remote and long-term. By directly confronting the external forces of change and negotiating with them on basic economic, social, and political matters, the Dene are seeking a permanent solution.

Appendix A

Transcription of a Song

Song 1 as performed at the Christmas Drum Dance

Appendix B

Melodic Sketches

Song 1

Song 2

Song 3

Song 4   No melodic transcription

Song 5

102 • Appendix B

Song 6

Song 7

Song 8

Song 9

Song 10

Song 11

Song 12   No melodic transcription

104 • *Appendix B*

Song 19

Song 20

Song 21

Song 22

Appendix C

Implications of Dene Kinship for the Structuralist Paradigm

Lévi-Strauss's division of social structures into elementary, Crow-Omaha, and complex types may be envisioned in a table where one axis is labelled descent and the other is labelled marriage rules. Each axis contains two divisions: for descent, they are unilineal and non-unilineal; for marriage rules, they are "positive marriage rule systems" and "negative marriage rule systems." The primary focus of Lévi-Strauss's *Elementary Structures of Kinship* (1969) is on societies that have unilineal descent and positive marriage rules; he labels these elementary structures. Elementary structures are of two basic kinds: those with restricted, or direct, exchange rules and those with generalized, or indirect, exchange rules. Lévi-Strauss further subdivides each of these into various specific types such as moiety and section, matrilateral and patrilateral. The second fundamental kind of social structure identified by Lévi-Strauss (1966) is Crow-Omaha; these societies have unilineal descent but negative marriage rules (see Lathrop 1978 for a different view). The third type of social structure is identified as complex. These are societies that have non-unilineal descent and negative marriage rules, for example, Euro-Canadian society.

The above analysis, when structured as a table, reveals an empty cell for the category of *no unilineal descent and positive marriage rules*. This category, which has never been postulated hypothetically nor described in the ethnographic literature, can be labelled Bilateral-Dravidianate.[1]

Because of the apparent absence of unilineality and positive marriage rules, Slavey Dene band composition, marriage, and kinship nomenclature appear to conform to Lévi-Strauss's complex type of social structure. However, the data presented here indicate that, while descent is not unilineal, there is an underlying tendency toward a positive marriage rule. These data include: the binary nature of the kinship structure; the use of Dravidian-type terminology; the structural opposition between cross and parallel cousins; and informal statements and behaviours which sanction certain classes of marriage, in particular between individuals classed as cross-cousins. Since, in terms of both marriage classification and terminological structure, the Pe Tsʼéh Kį́ Dene also resemble the Dravidian model (Dumont 1953), they can therefore be seen as having a bilateral descent system with a Dravidian-type structure, referred to here as Bilateral-Dravidianate.

This analysis may also apply to much of the kinship and ethnographic data reported by Helm (MacNeish 1960, Helm 1961) for various Mackenzie Drainage communities, by Ridington (1969) for the Beaver Dene, and even among the Xingu Carib of South America (Basso 1970 and Dole 1969). This interpretation is supported by the detailed analysis of the kinship terminology, marriage rules, and band composition of Beaver and Slavey, as well as other Dene or Athapaskan-speaking peoples, undertaken in Ives's dissertation *Northern Athapaskan Social and Economic Variability* (1985).

In conclusion, a fourth type of social structure, Bilateral-Dravidianate, is postulated. Where it exists, it is postulated that variability will be organized around the opposition between those societies, like the Slavey Dene with band exogamy and those like the Beaver Dene with band endogamy.

Footnotes

1. After Trautmann (1981:237) who uses "Dravidianate" to distinguish the structural type of kinship from any historically based connection with a particular South Indian group that the use of "Dravidian" might imply.

Appendix D

Some Conclusions on Music Analysis

One objective of this study was to test the utility of a model for music analysis, based on the hypothesis that a typological correlation exists between certain aspects of music sound and certain social behaviours: there is a positive correlation between form and function; and when function is defined on the basis of observed social behaviour and interviews, rather than on interviews alone, a more useful set of categories can be derived. The verbal statements and the social behaviours associated with Drum Dance music are demonstrated in the Rabbit Dances, Cree Dances, Tea Dances, Opening Songs, and Practice Songs. There are regularities in the relationship between tonal range, melodic structure, and rhythmic organization on the one hand; and their function, as described by the five types of social behavior, on the other. Therefore it is possible to derive culturally perceived, or emic, formal properties in music sound using descriptive linguistic methodology. This can be further tested in other research.

This finding also has interesting implications for the way in which Western scholars typically conceptualize the nature of music sound communication. The notion that musical utterances are produced either for purely formal considerations or to communicate on the psychological, emotional, or verbal level has led many to assume that the effects of musical communications cannot be observed. As a result, there has been a tendency to approach musical analysis on the basis of Euro-Canadian concepts of formal categories or, more recently, from interviews concerning the nature of music sound within a specific society. However, this has not proved to be a highly productive approach to the analysis of correlations between form and function.

This study challenges the above approach by postulating that observational parameters do exist by which functional categories can be isolated. Some aspects of music, like language, can have a denotative, communicative quality, one that is readily understood and responded to through appropriate behaviours by members of the musical community, or those who can differentiate the message from the sound. The use of this present approach in analyzing the Slavey Drum Dance music shows that such denotative components can be found in their music. The finding that there is a possible relationship between form and function in music which creates denotative meaning indicates that the analysis of music sound can follow the path already established for the analysis of the structure of language.

On the basis of this method, it appears that music structure parallels language structure in at least two ways, the first of which is further divisible into two categories: a phonetic — observer-based analysis of sound utilizing the notion of pitches — and a phonemic — an informant-based understanding of how sounds are utilized within the music and glossed as tones. Like phonemes, tones seem to be relative sound units in that their function is understood only in relation to other perceived sound units within a phonemic, or scale, system. This concept, however, has never been systematically used to assess the emically accurate basis of tone designations within a musical corpus. In this corpus an "allophonic" type variation was also found as when the tone B (using the tone G as the tonic) was preceded by the tone C it was always performed at a slightly lower pitch than when preceeded by any other tone. This lends further weight to the possibility that music sound production is similar to that used in producing sounds in speech.

Second, the formal-functional relationship itself seems to indicate that music may have properties similar to the morphemic ones found in language. Music sound production and the behaviours associated with it may be similar to the sound properties of a word and its denotative communicative function. Were this discovered to be the case in other musics, our understanding of how and what music communicates would be deepened by the creation of a method of music analysis as precise as that which now exists in the analysis of spoken language.

References Cited

Asch, Michael I.
(1972) *A social behavioral approach to the analysis of music: The case of the Slavey Drum Dance*. Unpublished doctoral dissertation. New York: Department of Anthropology, Columbia University.
(1973) *An Anthology of North American Indian and Eskimo Music* (two records and accompanying notes) -23-FE4541. New York: Folkways Records and Service Corporation.
(1975a) Social Context and the Musical Analysis of Slavey Drum Dance Songs. *Ethnomusicology* 19:245-267.
(1975b) Achieving the Ideal Drum Dance. Paper presented at the 1975 Annual Meeting of the American Folklore Society (unpublished manuscript).
(1976) Some Effects of the Late Nineteenth Century Modernization of the Fur Trade on the Economy of the Slavey Indians. *The Euro-Canadian Canadian Journal of Anthropology* VI:7-15.
(1977) The Dene Economy. *In* M. Watkins, *Dene Nation: The Colony Within*. Toronto: University of Toronto Press, pp. 47-61.
(1979) The Economics of Dene Self-determination. *In* D. Turner & G. Smith, editors, *Challenging Anthropology*. Toronto: McGraw-Hill Ryerson, pp. 339-352.
(1980) Steps Towards the Analysis of Aboriginal Athapaskan Social Organization. *Arctic Anthropology* 17(2):46-51.
(1981) The Slavey Indians. *In* J. Helm, editor, *The Handbook of North American Indians, Vol. 6: The Subarctic*. Washington, DC: The Smithsonian Institution.
(1982) Dene Self-determination and the Study of Hunter-Gatherers in the Modern World. *In* E. Leacock & R. B. Lee, editors, *Politics and History in Band Societies*. Cambridge: Cambridge University Press.
(1985) *Home and Native Land: Aboriginal Rights and the Canadian Constitution*. Toronto: Methuen of Canada.
(in press) The Slavey Indians: The Relevance of Ethnohistory to Development. *In* C.R. Wilson and R.B. Morrison, editors, *Native Peoples: The Canadian Experience*. Toronto: McClelland and Stewart, 40 p.

Basso, Ellen
(1970) Xingu Carib Kinship Terminology: Another View. *Southern Journal of Anthropology* 26:402-416.

Bethune, W.C.
(1937) *Canada's Northland*. Ottawa: King's Printer.

Bisset, D.
(1967) *The Lower Mackenzie Region: an Economic Survey*. Ottawa: Department of Indian Affairs and Northern Development.

Blacking, J.
(1967) *Venda Children's Songs*. Johannesburg: Witwatersrand University Press.
(1971) Deep and Surface Structures in Venda Music. *Yearbook of the International Folk Music Council* III:91-108.

Bodden, Kenneth R.
(1981) *The Economic Use by Native Peoples of the Resources of the Slave River Delta*. Edmonton: Unpublished Master of Arts Thesis, Department of Geography, University of Alberta.

Bompas, W.C.
(1888) *Diocese of Mackenzie River*. London: Society for Promoting Christian Knowledge.

Bright, W.
(1963) Language and Music: Areas for Cooperation. *Ethnomusicology* 7:26-32.

Dawson, C. A.
(1947) *The New Northwest*. Toronto: The University of Toronto Press.

Densmore, F.
(1918) *Teton Sioux Music*. Washington, DC: Bureau of American Ethnology Bulletin 61.

Dole, Gertrude
(1969) Generation Kinship Nomenclature as an Adaptation to Endogamy. *South Euro-Canadian Journal of Anthropology* 25:105-123.

Dumont, Louis
(1953) The Dravidian Kinship Terminology as an Expression of Marriage. *Man* 54:34-39.

Economic Staff Group and MPS Associates Ltd.
(1973) *Regional Impact of a Northern Gas Pipeline Vol. 5*. Ottawa: Northern Economic Development Branch, Department of Indian Affairs and Northern Development.

Feld, S.
(1974) Linguistic Models in Ethnomusicology. *Ethnomusicology* 18(2):197-217.

Freeman, L.C. and A.P. Merriam
(1956) Statistical Classification in Anthropology: An Application to Ethnomusicology. *American Anthropologist* 58:464-472.

Fumoleau, Rene
(1977) *As Long as This Land Shall Last*. Toronto: McClelland and Stewart.
(1984) Denendeh: A Dene Celebration. Yellowknife: The Dene Nation.

Goffman, Erving
(1961) Fun in Games. *In* E. Goffman, *Encounters: Two studies in the sociology of interaction*. Indianapolis: The Bobbs-Merrill Company, pp. 17-81.

Gove, P.B. (ed.)
(1966) *Webster's Third New International Dictionary*. Springfield: G. & C. Merriam Co.

Halliday, W.E.D.
(1937) *A Forest Classification for Canada*. Ottawa: King's Printer.

Harris, M.
(1964) *The Nature of Cultural Things*. New York: Random House.

Helm, June
(1961) *The Lynx Point People: The Dynamics of a Northern Athapaskan Band*. Ottawa: National Museum of Canada Bulletin 176.
(1961) *The Subsistence Economy of the Dog Rib of Lac La Matre in the Mackenzie District of the Northwest Territories*. Ottawa: Department of Northern Affairs and Natural Resources.
(1965) Bilaterality in the Socio-Territorial Organization of the Arctic Drainage Dene. *Ethnology* 4:361-385.
(1973) *Subarctic Athapaskan Bibliography*. Iowa City: Department of Anthropology, University of Iowa.

Helm, June (ed.)
(1981) *The Handbook of North American Indians; Vol. 6: The Subarctic.* Washington, DC: Smithsonian Institution.

Helm, June and R. Kurtz
(1984) *Subarctic Athapaskan Bibliography - 1984.* Iowa City: Department of Anthropology, University of Iowa.

Helm, June and N. Lurie
(1966) *The Dogrib Hand Game.* Ottawa: National Museum of Man.

Herndon, Marcia
(1971) The Cherokee Ballgame Cycle: An Ethnomusicologist's View. *Ethnomusicology* 15:339-352.

Honigmann, J. J.
(1946) *Ethnography and Acculturation of the Fort Nelson Slave.* New Haven: Yale University Publications in Anthropology 33.
(1949) *Culture and Ethos of Kaska Society.* New Haven: Yale University Publications in Anthropology 40.
(1954) *The Kaska Indians: An Ethnographic Reconstruction.* New Haven: Yale University Publications in Anthropology 51.

Hudson's Bay Company
(no date) Hudson's Bay Company Fact Sheet on Wrigley. (Unpublished mimeograph).

Ives, John W.
(1985) *Northern Athapaskan Social and Economic Variability.* Unpublished Doctoral Dissertation, Ann Arbor: Department of Anthropology, University of Michigan.

Janes, Robert
(1983) *Archaeological Ethnography among the Mackenzie Basin Dene, Canada.* Calgary: The Arctic Institute of North America, technical paper -23-28.

Kendrew, W.G. and B.W. Currie
(1955) *The Climate of Canada.* Ottawa: Queen's Printer.

Kolinski, M.
(1957) An Evaluation of Tempo. *Ethnomusicology* 3:45-57.
(1965) The Structure of Melodic Movement: A New Method of Analysis. *Studies in Ethnomusicology* 2:95-120.
(1967) Recent Trends in Ethnomusicology. *Ethnomusicology* 11:1-24.

Krech III, Shepard
(1984) The Trade of the Slavey and Dogrib at Fort Simpson in the early 19th century. *In* S. Krech, editor, *The Sub-Arctic Fur Trade: Native Social and Economic Adaptation.* Vancouver: University of British Columbia Press.

Kurath, Gertrude
(1966) Dog-Rib Choreography and Music. *In* J. Helm and N. Lurie, editors, *The Dog Rib Game.* Ottawa: National Museum of Man.

Lamb, W. Kaye (ed.)
(1970) *The Journals and Letters of Sir Alexander Mackenzie.* Toronto: Macmillan of Canada.

Lathrop, G. Mark
(1978) *A Solution to the Crow-Omaha Problem and its Implications for Future Research into Social Organization.* Unpublished Master of Arts thesis. Edmonton: Department of Anthropology, University of Alberta.

Lévi-Strauss, Claude
    (1966) The Future of Kinship Studies. *Proceedings of the Royal Anthropological Institute* 1965:13-22.
    (1969) *The Elementary Structures of Kinship.* London: Eyre and Spottiswoode.

Lyons, J.
    (1969) *Introduction to Theoretical Linguistics.* Cambridge: Cambridge University Press.

MacNeish, J. H.
    (1956) Leadership Among the Northeastern Athabascans. *Anthropologica* 2:131-163.
    (1960) Kin Terms of the Arctic Drainage Dene: Hare, Slavey, Chipewyan. *American Anthropologist* 62(2):279-295.

Mason, J. Aldon
    (1946) *Notes on the Indians of the Great Slave Lake Area.* New Haven: Yale University Publications in Anthropology -23-34.

McAllester, D.
    (1954) *Enemy Way Music.* Cambridge: Peabody Museum Papers 41(3), Harvard University Press.

McDonald, T.H.
    (1966) *Exploring the Northwest Territory.* Norman: University of Oklahoma Press.

McLeod, Norma and M. Herndon
    (1980) *The Ethnography of Musical Performance.* Norwood, PA:Norwood Editions.

Merriam, A.P.
    (1963) The Purpose of Ethnomusicology: An Anthropological View. *Ethnomusicology* 7:206-213.
    (1964) *The Anthropology of Music.* Evanston: North Euro-Canadian University Press.
    (1967) *Ethnomusicology of the Flathead Indians.* New York: Viking Fund Publications in Anthropology 44.

Murphy, Robert
    (1971) *The Dialectics of Social Life: Alarms and Excursions in Anthropological Theory.* New York: Basic Books.

Nattiez, Jean-Jacques
    (1975) *Fondements d'une seminiologie de la Musique.* Paris: Seuil.

Nettl, B.
    (1964) *Theory and Method in Ethnomusicology.* Glencoe: Free Press.

Osgood, G.
    (1936) *The Distribution of Northern Athapaskan Tribes.* New Haven: Yale University Publications in Anthropology 7.
    (1940) *Ingalik Material Culture.* New Haven: Yale University Publications in Anthropology 22.

Pike, K.
    (1954) *Language in Relation to a Unified Theory of the Structure of Human Behavior.* Summer Institute of Linguistics 1.

Qureshi, Regula
    (1981) *Qawnali: Sound, Context and Meaning in Indo-Muslim Sofi Music.* Unpublished Ph.D. dissertation. Edmonton: Department of Anthropology, University of Alberta.

Rhodes, W.
    (1958) A Study of Musical Diffusion Based on the Wandering of the Opening Peyote Song. *Journal of the International Folk Music Council* 10:42-49.

Ridington, Robin
  (1969) Kin Categories vs. Kin Groups: A Two Section System without Sections. *Ethnology* 8:460-467.
Roberts, H.
  (1936) *Musical Areas in Aboriginal North America.* New Haven: Yale University Publications in Anthropology 11.
Russell, R.
  (1898) *Explorations in the Far North.* Ames: University of Iowa.
Savishinsky, Joel
  (1974) *The Trail of the Hare: Life and Stress in an Arctic Community.* New York: Gordon and Breach Science Publishers.
Shapiro, Warren
  (1970) The Ethnography of Two-Section Systems. *Ethnology* 9:380-388.
Slobodin, R.
  (1962) *Band Organization of the Peel River Kutchin.* Ottawa: National Museum of Canada 179.
Spier, Leslie
  (1925) The Distribution of Kinship System in North America. *University of Washington Publications in Anthropology*, Vol. 1, -23-2:71-88. Seattle: University of Washington.
Springer, G.
  (1956) Language and Music: Parallels and Divergencies. *In* M. Halle, editor, *For Ramon Jakobson.* 's-Gravenhage: Mouton.
Stewart, E.
  (1913) *Down the Mackenzie and Up the Yukon in 1906.* London.
Sturtevant, W.
  (1964) Studies in Ethnoscience. *American Anthropologist* 66(3) Part 2: 99-131.
Taylor, G.
  (1947) A Mackenzie Domesday: 1944. *In* C. A. Dawson, editor, *The New Northwest.* Toronto: University of Toronto.
Trautmann, Thomas
  (1981) *Dravidian Kinship.* Cambridge: Cambridge University Press.
Waldo, F.
  (1923) *Down the Mackenzie River.* New York: Macmillan.
Watkins, Mel
  (1977) *Dene Nation: The Colony Within.* Toronto: University of Toronto Press.
Willey, G.R.
  (1966) *An Introduction to American Archeology V. 1.* Englewood Cliffs: Prentice-Hall.